Writing Historical Novels

Studymates

British History 1870–1918
Warfare 1792–1918
Hitler and Nazi Germany (3rd Edition)
English Reformation
European History 1870–1918
Genetics (2nd edition)
Lenin, Stalin and Communist Russia
Organic Chemistry
Chemistry: As Chemistry Explained
Chemistry: Chemistry Calculations Explained
The New Science Teacher's Handbook
Mathematics for Adults
Calculus
Understanding Forces
Algebra: Basic Algebra Explained
Plant Physiology
Poems to Live By
Shakespeare
Poetry
Better English
Better French
Better German
Better Spanish
Social Anthropology
Statistics for Social Science
Practical Drama and Theatre Arts
The War Poets 1914–18
The Academic Essay
Your Master's Thesis
Your PhD Thesis

Studymates

Helping You to Achieve

Writing Historical Novels

Marina Oliver

© 2005 by Marina Oliver

ISBN 10 1-84 285-077-6
ISBN 13 978 1-84 285-077-0

First published in 2005 by Studymates Limited.
PO Box 225, Abergele, LL18 9AY, United Kingdom.

Website: http://www.studymates.co.uk

Typeset by Domex e-Data Pvt. Ltd.
Printed and bound in Great Britain by Baskerville Press

Contents

4 Characters 1 – people are same the world over 53

5 Characters 2 – circumstances change 69

Foreword

There are two popularly held misconceptions about historical fiction.

The first is that it is fashionable, or unfashionable. In reality, there is a remarkably consistent output. Each year the Historical Novel Society reviews around 800 newly published titles – which is a vast number for any genre. There are also many first-time authors finding publishers each year. It is certainly true that there are fashions within the genre in different years and different countries, but the overall popularity of historical fiction does not change.

The second misconception is that historical fiction is easier, or more difficult, to write than 'normal' fiction. Those who think it is easier are usually convincing themselves that they do not need to make up a story because the story is already there for them; those who think it more difficult are usually daunted by research. In reality historical fiction absolutely depends on the author's ability to tell a new story, and all novels depend on research. Historical fiction is neither easier nor more difficult, but it is different, and hence the need for *Writing Historical Fiction*.

In clear, no-nonsense format, Marina Oliver tackles each of the challenges of the genre head-on. She balances advice on technique with encouragement for inspiration, and wryly sounds warning notes against the pitfalls and 'howlers' of the genre.

For me, the invaluable part of this guide is that along with the advice there are practical, helpful exercises to attempt. I challenge any new writer to finish this book and pick up a blank sheet of paper and to find that it remains blank. *Writing Historical Fiction* will also help you with blocks along the way and, most usefully, gives advice on how to get your work published.

I recommend it whole-heartedly.

Richard Lee
Founder/Publisher *The Historical Novel Society*

Preface

The growth of local history societies, re-enactment groups, living history museums, and genealogical research, as well as the popularity of costume drama on TV, indicates that many people have an interest in some form of history in a palatable form. History combined with storytelling skills can be a wonderful experience. Historical fiction of all sorts has immense appeal.

Writing historical novels requires the same techniques as for any novel, characterisation, plotting and so on, but in addition when writing historical fiction there is the need to combine historical facts with the story. A novel is more appealing if it is not a disguised textbook, so how can writers of historical fiction include what is necessary and interesting without overdoing the historical facts? This is what I hope to show you in this guide.

Some historical novels are in reality little more than any story in fancy dress, with little historical detail and sometimes little historical understanding. At the opposite extreme, others often read like biographies. All have a place, and just as readers of crime fiction have preferences for, let's say, police procedurals rather than female private eyes, readers can prefer one type of historical novel to another. There is plenty of scope for writers and I hope this book will help aspiring authors to become published historical novelists.

Don't be overwhelmed by the task in front of you. There is a great deal to consider and you won't be able to recall all of it at once. Some of the things I suggest are alternatives, some depend on how far your story is embedded in historical fact. Read published novels, analyse them, and learn from their examples how they apply the techniques I describe here.

Marina Oliver

1 The joys of historicals

What is a novel?

A novel is a work of fiction, where the author uses his or her imagination to create a story. There is usually some relation to fact in all novels, if only a specific, real or invented location or institution against which the story is set. Historical novels use facts from former times and weave them into the imaginary story.

Most novelists say they write to entertain and because they enjoy the process of creation. Some use the novel form to explore ideas, create new worlds or look at our world from a new angle. Novels vary from the simple, straightforward story to the complex exploration of ideas. This gives scope for a wonderful variety, and you, as creator, can choose your own form.

Historical novels vary as much as any other type, apart from being set in a real, former time. So what makes a novel a historical?

What is an historical novel?

At first this appears to be a simple question. Surely a historical novel is a work of fiction set in the past? Ask yourself, what counts as 'the past'? Strictly, yesterday is 'the past', but novels set in very recent times are never marketed as historicals. Also, many novels set in the past are not marketed as historicals, but as other genres.

Don't be misled by descriptions

Some novels I would define as historicals are marketed, for a different audience, under other descriptions. In the *Guardian* list of fast-selling paperbacks for 2002, for example, Charlotte Bingham's *Chestnut Tree* was described as 'Novel', but it was set in the Second World War.

The following are some descriptions from a database, which is a marketing tool used by publishers, and gives the genre of the novel. Most historical crime was listed as just crime. Others were described not as historical, but modern (eg Iris Gower's *Copper Kingdom*, Louis de Berniere's *Captain Corelli's Mandolin*, Robert Graves's *I Claudius*, John Fowles's *French Lieutenant's Woman*, Sebastian Faulkes's *Birdsong*), or war fiction (Bernard Cornwell's *Sharpe's Eagle*), adventure/ thriller (Iain Pears's *An Instance of the Fingerpost*, and G. Macdonald Fraser's *Flashman*).

Historicals are perhaps regarded by publishers as unpopular, so a cynical piece of advice is to try and market it to an agent as something else!

So where can we draw the line?

Before what date can we describe a book as 'historical'? All the above examples, which are labelled as something else, were set during the Second World War or earlier – much earlier, some of them. The cut-off point is a question which causes debate when prizes are being offered, and the answers are various and pretty arbitrary. For several decades the Second World War used to be a regular cut-off point, but now, in the twenty-first century, this point has moved closer to the millennium. It has much to do with the editors who were born long after 1945, as well as readers. Many people would define a historical novel as 'before I was born', so this could vary by a hundred years.

Does it matter, as long as your novel is set in the past? You will be safe to describe your novel as a historical if it is set fifty or more years ago.

Imagination and fact

Historical novels vary from those with an immense amount of factual detail, often based on the life of a real person, such as those by Jean Plaidy, to those which simply use the background in which to place purely imaginary characters. We will look at the many types later.

If featuring a real personage, what makes novels different from a straight biography? The answer is imagination. The biographer deals with a whole life, verified facts and his interpretation of them. The novelist may take a slice of that life and invent what he cannot know, such as conversations and actions never recorded, but which could have taken place.

Pleasure for readers

Historicals have an enduring appeal for readers. Any good novel will give the reader a glow of satisfaction or make them think. We read novels for escapism, enjoyment and often for knowledge. The knowledge might be about people in general, what makes them tick, or places.

Reading historical novels is a way of learning about history in a very palatable manner. Often the history taught in school has been boring or disjointed, or concentrates on the twentieth century, and when they are older people may feel they want to know more, without making it an academic study.

Knowledge for readers

Readers may feel virtuous by acquiring knowledge, and since many people still regard reading fiction as a waste of time, we avid readers often feel the need to justify ourselves. Many historicals contain high adventure, or romance in the widest definition. Those set in more recent times may portray a way of life older readers can remember or have been told about by their parents, so there is nostalgia too.

Storytellers have always told about history

In prehistoric times there were no written records, but everywhere tribes had storytellers. These people, learning and passing on oral history, often described as the collective consciousness of the tribe, were honoured, important and respected members of the tribe. They told of the tribe's past, how they came to be and ancestors' valiant deeds of which the tribe could be proud. They also used stories to teach proper behaviour and warn about the penalties of unsocial actions. These may have been based on real events, or could be what we would now call fables or morality tales.

Classical writers and examples

Historical, written fiction existed in pre-Classical times, as we can see from fragments of novels found in ancient Egypt. Some of these were novels in prose form, but poetry and drama have also played their part. Many of these stories were about historical events. Homer's *Illiad* was once thought to be imaginary.

Knights errant

The 'romances' of the troubadours and Malory's tales of King Arthur are perhaps the best-known examples of stories set in the past but written during medieval times.

Recent times

Academics argue about the beginnings of the novel, and usually cite Daniel Defoe as the first modern English novelist. From his time the novel has flourished, and many authors have set some of their books in the past. It's a long tradition.

It is not only novelists who trawl history for subjects. Playwrights from Shakespeare on have used historical events or times for their work. Even before Shakespeare, medieval miracle plays often related biblical stories, and even further back some of the classical Greek dramas were historical.

This is not, however, a list of past historical novelists or playwrights. Interesting though many of them are to read, you won't learn much from them about how to write a saleable novel for today's market. It is an illustration of how history has always had appeal.

Today's publishers demand a different style, a new approach. The leisurely descriptions of Victorian novelists take too long for modern readers, used to the rapid scene changes of radio and TV drama.

The attempt to render speech in what was thought to be the contemporary idiom, which some nineteenth-century novelists did, can be excruciatingly difficult to understand and is now frowned upon.

Twentieth-century favourites

However, some historical novelists who were published in the first half or middle of the twentieth century can still teach us something. For example, you can study how they plot the story, insert appropriate historical details, use language and dialogue, or construct a succession of stories where the books can both stand alone and yet be part of a series.

Their novels remain as fresh today as when they were written, continually finding new readers, and with new editions regularly published.

The prime example, perhaps, is Georgette Heyer, whose skill in plotting, use of historical language, and knowledge of the Regency period, are unsurpassed. Then there is Dorothy Dunnett, whose books are full of wonderful detail.

Norah Lofts often set novels with a particular house as an important character, or wrote series based on them.

Winston Graham's *Poldark* series, featuring the same group of people became, immensely popular after television exposure.

Modern writers

You will no doubt have your own favourites and the following is by no means an exhaustive list of novelists writing historicals today. I mention them in order to illustrate the vast range of options for your own novels.

Writers need to read

You cannot hope to be a successful novelist unless you read novels extensively and widely. Don't read just the sort of books you want to write, though you need to read these to see what is being published. Read all kinds of novels. As you write, be critical, and look for good (and sometimes bad!) examples of what published writers do and how they achieve their effects.

Types and authors

There are many different types of historical novels and it's not always easy to categorise them into narrow definitions, but there are some broad categories with certain similarities. If you don't already know these authors, try their books.

Male appeal

Men often prefer novels of action, and a military or naval background can provide this. Many of the authors who specialise in these types of books are immensely knowledgeable.

The best known, perhaps, are Bernard Cornwell with his Sharpe novels set in the time of the Napoleonic wars, the hero a rifleman, and C. S. Forester and Patrick O'Brien with their naval stories. They have all been writing for many years.

A relative newcomer with a growing reputation is Allan Mallinson, who sets his books around a company of Light Dragoons in the years after Waterloo, with much detail about horses.

High adventure

Wilbur Smith's books, of adventure and family fortunes, have a huge appeal for both men and women. They are less easily classified, being more varied, but they are mainly adventure stories, many set in Africa.

For early medieval adventure try Elizabeth Chadwick, who sets her novels with many different backgrounds and some of her later novels based on the lives of real people. She is brilliant at making the historical details of everyday life an integral part of the story. There are also Sharon Penman and Roberta Gellis who have set books during this period.

Wartime

There have been hundreds of books set in the First and Second World Wars and the American Civil War, many of which might be called sagas, or be parts of series. I wrote several books with English Civil War backgrounds. Some others, such as Sebastian Faulks' *Birdsong* and Louis de Bernieres' *Captain Corelli's Mandolin* have been marketed more as literary novels than historicals.

Series

Cynthia Harrod-Eagles has written a very successful *Dynasty* series, the books set at different times from the Wars of the Roses, but all featuring the Morland family.

Mary Jane Staples has written more than two dozen books about the Adams family from Walworth, South London. These are concentrated in a smaller timespan, covering the first half of the twentieth century.

Alex Stuart's series, *The Australians*, which she wrote under the male pseudonym William Stuart Long, covers the settlement of the country.

Sagas

This is a fairly comprehensive term which covers a wide range of novels. Many so described are based on a family, but there are other backgrounds. They are usually set in the eighteenth, nineteenth and early twentieth centuries, often featuring a particular region.

Emma Blair, Josephine Cox, Iris Gower, Audrey Howard, Anna Jacobs, Elvi Rhodes, Wendy Robertson, Susan Sallis and many other writers use this form. Sometimes the books are independent, but often there are several following the lives of one family, or different members of the family and their neighbours, and these can overlap with the former classification of series.

Regencies

Regency novels have a small but devoted following in the USA and elsewhere, but only a few publishers still take them. The typical 'Regency' is a comedy of manners, such as Georgette Heyer wrote, but now they often feature older heroines and more serious problems, and some of the American versions are more raunchy than the archetypal 'Regency' used to be. Try the Harlequin authors Joanna Maitland and Nicola

Cornick, and the British-born Jo Beverley, who lives in Canada and wrote many 'Regencies' for American imprints.

Biographical

Jean Plaidy excelled in this sort of novel, where a real person is the hero or heroine. A recent example is Phillipa Gregory's *The Other Boleyn Girl*.

Crime

Historical crime has been a growing area. Ellis Peters started it off with the Cadfael novels, and many crime novelists have followed her. Lindsey Davis, with her ancient Roman hero Falco, is well known, but there are many others such as Elizabeth Peters with her female sleuth Amelia Peabody, Kate Sedley, Susanna Gregory and Michael Jecks writing about medieval times. P. C. Doherty, Peter Lovesey and Edward Marston all have a variety of settings from ancient Egypt to the Second World War. The sleuths are usually fictional, but some authors use a real character as the detective hero. Margaret Doody has featured Aristotle, and Janet Lawrence the artist Canaletto.

Children's historicals

These are growing in popularity, and there are as many types in this market as for adult fiction. One trend here is to choose settings with regard to National Curriculum topics.

Others

The above are perhaps the main classifications, but there are many sub-genres. Gothics, with, usually, a solitary girl in an isolated, forbidding house, have gone out of fashion, as have the more violent bodice-rippers. Period novels often have only a nodding acquaintance with historical fact.

Westerns are popular in the USA, but are changing from the old style. Recent novels have been epics, with a large canvas spanning several generations. They have been taking new angles, with the emphasis on social history rather than political, and frequently showing events from the female or native point of view.

Novels of the paranormal are becoming increasingly popular. This overlaps with time-slip novels, and Barbara Erskine and Diana Gabaldon are well-known writers in this field.

Less easy to classify are authors such as Philip Pullman and Matthew Kneale, both multiple prize-winners. Philip Pullman is best known for his fantasy trilogy, but was well established before this writing historicals for young adults. Matthew Kneale has written a variety of historicals, the best known the prize-winning *English Passengers*.

American preferences

In general, there are more 'fancy-dress' historicals in the USA than in England. English and Scottish settings are popular. In those which have a more solid historical setting, American readers prefer real characters and a wide canvas and involvement in important events.

In both they prefer characters who are aristocratic, not middle or working class.

Take your choice

You will have your own preferences and skills, and this book will help you to define them and aim towards the most likely chance of publication.

Pleasures for writers

Why should you choose to write historical novels? Are they more difficult? Yes, in some ways, but they also have advantages.

In writing historicals you need the same skills as for any other novels, plus the ability to do research. This is absolutely essential, and you need to be prepared for it and to enjoy doing it as much as you enjoy writing.

There is, of course, some research needed for all novels, but usually far more for historicals. This is part of the pleasure for many writers, though many admit they are often carried away and pursue avenues that are nothing to do with their current book but intrinsically fascinating.

In the same way that readers may be seeking escapism by imagining they are living in the past, writers like to do the same.

From a practical point of view, it is easier to write a series of novels set in the past than a series set in the present. Series can be profitable for writers once they acquire a faithful readership, and the settings can move forward in time almost indefinitely.

Unlimited scope

Then there is the possibility of endless variety of time and place from which the novelist can choose. We have the whole of history and the entire human race to explore. Some writers confine themselves to one period, others have settings from different times.

The challenge of combining imagination with real events

For many writers, the challenge of combining imagination with real events adds a fascinating dimension to the plotting of novels. The plot must be carefully devised to fit the known facts. This is understandably trickier than having total freedom to invent the facts, but many writers find it an enormously satisfying exercise.

Below is a brief, simplified extract from the chart I kept when writing *The Cobweb Cage*. I show here columns for two of the characters, and rows for the years. I noted both local and national events which I might mention or incorporate into my plot. For instance, one of the sisters sulks because she wants to go on the Sunday school treat, thus showing her nature. I have someone mention Bleriot because Richard becomes a pilot during the war, so it foreshadows the notion of flying. The local racehorse provides a reason for Richard's visit to the town, to see his father's horses in training.

Year	Marigold	Ivy	Local events	National events
1908	helps at home		Colliery fire	
1909		accident, burned	Sunday school treat	Bleriot flies Channel, General election
1910	leaves school	begins school	Local horse wins Grand National	Edward VIII dies
1914	marries Richard		Chasetown RAMC leave for military service	War begins
1915	Widowed son born		Tackeroo railway line built	

Questions to answer and things to do

Off the top of your head, and without looking anything up:

1. List your five favourite historical novels.

   Are they of the same type or by the same author? Are they set in one period, or even the same century?

2. List your five favourite authors of historical novels.

   Do they write varied books or are they similar in type or period?

3. What is your favourite historical period? And why?

   It may be the First World War, the Victorian or Tudor era, or Ancient Britain. Is it your favourite because you already know a lot about it, or would have liked to live then?

4. Write a page of notes on what you know about this period.

   Include such things as which dynasty or king is on the throne, wars taking place, trends, religious beliefs and influences, social life, politics, science, technology, medicine, art and architecture.

5. Who is your favourite real historical person?

   Is he or she well known? The same sex as you? (Sometimes writers find it difficult to get into the other sex's mind.) Is this character from your favourite historical period? Have you read accounts of his or her life? Biographies? Novels featuring him or her?

6. Write a page of notes on what you know about this person.

For example, you may know their dates, family background, marriage, children, career, where they lived, the cause of their death (execution, battle, assassination, illness?)

7. Who is your favourite fictional historical character?

Is this from your favourite book or author?

8. Do your answers to the above indicate what sort of novels you will probably write and the period you are likely to set them in? For instance, do you concentrate on a particular time or place, one century, one country, the same kind of book or background, such as military, or featuring royalty? Have you been influenced by television programmes or films, either adaptations of novels or documentaries?

9 Put down one idea, or several, briefly outlining a novel you would like to write.

Tips by example

Here I will suggest a couple of ideas, and we will follow them briefly throughout the book.

1. A novel featuring one real historical person, Samuel Pepys, and his life during the first few years of his famous diary.

This has the advantage that we have an enormous amount of detail available from his own pen. There can be a lot of historical allusion because he was very involved in the politics of the day, close to the Restoration Court and knowledgeable about the navy and the Dutch Wars. We need to find a theme on which to structure the novel.

2. A family saga set in a particular period, the 1950s.

The advantage of this choice of time is that you may have lived through it, or have older relatives who did or know other people who can give you information. Let us have as our main characters three girls from different backgrounds, with different ambitions. For instance,

Marion could be a girl whose father made a fortune during the Second World War, perhaps in rather dubious ways. Her family want her to make a wealthy marriage but she wants to have a career.

Secondly, we could have Peggy, whose father was reported missing during the war, and she cannot move on until she knows what happened to him.

Thirdly, we might have Jennifer, a girl from a poor family who wants to go to university but her parents are against it. They all face problems.

Key points

1. Historicals are popular with readers.
2. They give pleasure and knowledge to both readers and writers.
3. Read as much as you can of all sorts of books.

Be a professional – you're a writer

Believe and act like a professional

Professionals get paid. Yes, and you hope to be paid for writing, but as yet your novel is still waiting to be written. So far you have not been paid. So how can you be a professional?

It can be shown in your attitude towards your work, which means you have to be determined, committed, and self-disciplined. Your writing is a job, not a hobby, and you need to treat it as such.

Decide how you'll work

This involves things such as whether you will work directly onto a word processor or write by hand, where you will work and when. There is no one method that is the best. Try different things until you find the one that suits you. This involves both the practical details of handwriting or word-processing, but also the imaginative process, such as how much to plan ahead.

Many writers start with pen or pencil. With pencils you can erase and change, but eventually a script must be typed, preferably word-processed. A professional typing agency is expensive. You will have so many changes, some major, especially after revision, that a handwritten script can become difficult to read. On a clean, newly printed copy, which you can do however many times you wish on a word processor, it is far easier to see mistakes and make judgements about the quality and rightness of your work.

Need for computers

If you don't already have one, it will be much cheaper and probably quicker to buy a computer and learn to type, than pay someone else to do it. A personal computer can also be used for making notes, keeping diaries, doing accounts and researching information via the Internet.

A small computer and simple word-processing program may be enough for you, but good print quality is important. You can skimp on the computer but buy the best printer you can afford.

Inkjet printers are cheap to buy, and you can use colour, but they are expensive to run. If you are going to be producing several printed drafts of your script, which many writers do, consider buying a laser printer. They are more expensive initially, and colour lasers are very expensive at the moment, but the running costs per sheet of paper are lower than for inkjets. Also compare running costs for different models as they vary considerably.

Publishers are increasingly asking for scripts, once accepted, to be sent to them on a disk. This saves them the cost of typesetting, since all the designer has to do is add the preliminary pages, reformat your text to the publisher's house style and set the pages. If you cannot comply it might make selling your novel more difficult, though not impossible.

Explore different methods

Finding out what suits your circumstances and creativity is a learning process which will make future writing easier and more efficient. Different methods suit different writers. You can start with a situation and characters and let them take over, going where they choose, or work out a detailed plan beforehand.

You can approach a project by working it all out in your head beforehand. Lots of writers do this, and find it helps them to see a way forward. Many of them, however, say they change things as they write the chapters.

You could write a few notes first, maybe just an outline of the first chapter or two, and expand on this as you write, making notes of the next chapter and so on. Perhaps you would feel more secure by writing detailed notes first, about all sorts of things as well as the plot. It can help you to immerse yourself in the period, feel your way, get to know your characters and the setting.

Many authors write a summary or synopsis first, and agents and publishers often want to see one, once they have accepted the first novel, for the second. We'll look at how to do this later, but it is a difficult skill to acquire. Many authors confess to writing their synopses after they have finished the novel.

You can take a couple of characters and an opening situation then just begin writing and see where it takes you. Character-driven plots are often written this way, but for inexperienced writers it could be difficult, you might run out of ideas if you haven't thought more about it to begin with.

You may be the sort of writer who is constantly redrafting as you go. I know some who have to have each page, every sentence and word absolutely correct before they can move on to the next. Many writers say they read through and correct what they have done the previous day, and this allows for some editing but also gets them back into the story. Or you may be one who prefers to do the redrafting after finishing a first attempt. These writers ignore small mistakes, typing errors and so on, until they have the whole story in draft form.

A few people can write scenes out of chronological order, as they think of them, or perhaps doing the big scenes first, and slot them into the right place later on.

As a beginner, writing your first lengthy project, you may feel happier to know that you can write a whole novel before you want to start revising it.

Books and magazines

Writers need all sorts of books. You will probably have some already, but obtaining others need not cost a lot. General reference books are invaluable. Second-hand copies are often perfectly adequate and can be found very cheaply. Also browse in remainder shops where glossy books on various topics are sold off at a fraction of their original price.

It's amazing how often writers need to consult dictionaries for the exact meanings of words, or *Roget's Thesaurus* for slightly different or more precise words. A spelling dictionary is quicker when all you want to check is a spelling. You'll probably want books on grammar, a small encyclopaedia and an atlas to provide valuable information such as time zones and weather patterns.

You may want specialised dictionaries such as historical slang, synonyms and foreign phrases. Other books worth collecting, especially by fiction writers, are dictionaries of quotations, books of names, books on furniture, costume and houses, second-hand copies of *Who's Who?* and *Whitaker's Almanack*, hotel and tourist guides, and maps.

A current yearbook such as *The Writers' and Artists' Yearbook* or *The Writer's Handbook*, or in the USA the *Writer's Market*, will become essential in time, but for now a recent second-hand copy will give you an idea of what they contain.

You will probably have books on subjects that interest you and know about the standard reference sources. You will need to consult reference books in libraries, but it is convenient to have frequently used books at home. For reference books on new subjects, and a quick overall view of a topic, books for children are useful.

There are several magazines for writers. The best known in the UK are *Writer's News*, which incorporates *Writing Magazine*, *Writer's Forum*, *The New Writer* and *Mslexia*. There are many others published in America, some of which can be obtained in the UK in very large bookshops such as Borders. Many of these magazines are available on subscription, a few can be found on newsagents' shelves. Get sample copies and see which appeals to you most before taking out a subscription.

Practise

Writing is a craft and needs to be learnt, just as much as painting or playing a musical instrument does. We can all splash paint on canvas, but can we produce a picture someone will want to buy? We can strike piano keys, but are we proficient enough to perform in public? These skills need practice, and so do all forms of writing. You also need to persevere, and to set yourself some kind of target.

Plan when and for how long each day or week you will write

Set yourself targets. It may be possible to write only at weekends, or find time by giving up other activities. Make time by watching less TV, skimping the housework, or getting up early.

The important thing is to find a routine which fits your circumstances, and to write regularly. If you have another job you will have to fit your writing around the job and family commitments, but this is how most writers began. It takes time to generate any income from writing.

Only when fully established or receiving a separate income can writers afford to give up the day job. When they do, they may have set times for writing, every morning or afternoon, or from 9.00 a.m. to 6.00 p.m. six days a week.

Others spend however long it takes to write 4–500 or 1,000 words each day.

Some write as long as they physically can when ideas are flowing, or set deadlines for completing a chapter, book or article. It may be a chapter a week or a page a day. It doesn't matter which method you choose as long as it works for you.

Fit in with your own life

Choose the best time for you. The time of day may depend on whether you are a lark or an owl. Many writers get up early and write before they go to work. Others work when everyone else is in bed. Some write during lunch breaks and any small lengths of spare time. Others can write during train journeys, perhaps while commuting to work.

Some days other commitments make even half an hour impossible. It helps to aim for a set number of hours or words per week. If one day or week is exceptionally busy, make up the time later – or in advance.

Be realistic, though. Don't aim too high at first. If you fail to keep to an unrealistic, demanding schedule you may well become disheartened and give up. Writing 1,000 words a day will enable you to write the first draft of a 90,000 word novel – the average length – in three months and 1,000 words is roughly four pages of A4, double-spaced text. And this is only typing at a speed of 16–17 words per minute for an hour. Of course, you probably won't type so rapidly because you will need time to think and plan, but it shows how little time is actually needed to complete a first draft.

Once you have this first draft you will probably spend an equal amount of time – perhaps twice as long – revising, rewriting and polishing. Many authors can write two books a year, most do only one.

Make a place of your own

This isn't absolutely essential but it helps enormously, even if it is just a small table in your bedroom. You'll feel in the mood for writing when you go there.

You could create a space by rearranging the furniture. Perhaps you could convert an attic or the cupboard under the stairs (but make sure you have sufficient ventilation!) With adequate heating, a garden shed or outhouse might be usable. Many writers like a separate 'office', a situation which makes them feel they are 'at work', and where they can be alone while doing their work.

Keep it to yourself

Once you have such a space, keep it for yourself. Some people can write at the kitchen table in the midst of family life, but most need more peace and isolation. Tell the family it is where you work, and encourage them not to interrupt when you are there. Make it clear to everyone that writing is a job, and interruptions damage your creativity and the flow of thought and ideas.

However small it is try to arrange all you need, such as vital reference books, pens, paper and notes, within reach. Include a comfortable chair for when you are reading, and good lighting at both your desk and chair. Reading, for research and revising, is essential but does not have to be done sitting at a desk.

Organise your space

Do you have adequate storage space for paper, notes, reference books, manuscripts and magazines? Eventually you will need far more than your first estimates of bookshelves, desk drawers, filing cabinets and cupboards.

It helps to have the most frequently used reference books close to hand, but you don't need everything in or by your desk – just the ones you use most often.

Improvisation

It's luxurious to have every variety of sophisticated office storage facility, but you can do it cheaply or improvise.

You can make bookshelves with bricks and planks to fit awkward places.

To store hanging or envelope files get appropriate sized, strong and deep cardboard boxes from supermarkets.

You can make dividers from sheets of stiff cardboard, or make folders with large old envelopes or paper bags.

Label everything in prominent letters.

Buy typing or computer paper in packs of five hundred sheets, or boxes of five packs: this is cheaper, and the boxes make ideal trays or storage containers.

Efficiency

You will need a method of keeping track of your submissions, and of earnings and expenses. Two readily handy notebooks may be the easiest for this. List any query letters or submissions you send, the dates sent and what reply you receive.

Survey your resources

Note what you already have, such as reference books, bookshelves and filing space, and make plans of what would be useful now or in the near future. Perhaps you can ask for whatever you need as a birthday present.

Plan your record system

Devise a filing system early on. You may file alphabetically, or keep notes on various subjects separate from letters or notes about markets. Start simply: too complicated a system can be confusing.

As you collect ideas, reference material and notes, you can expand your system for your new needs. File your notes regularly, in too many rather than too few separate files. We will look at some of the advantages and disadvantages of the different methods later.

Writing away from your desk

Writing time does not have to be spent at the keyboard, so most people can do an hour or two each day. You don't need a pen to 'write'. The term 'writing' can be misleading. It isn't just the time spent with a pen or keyboard, you need time for thinking and planning. Much of this can be done productively while you are on trains, walking the dog or washing up.

Making notes and plans is part of the writing process. For historicals especially, doing research is essential.

Then a good deal of time has to be spent revising what is already written.

Published writers have to read proofs and attend press and publicity events. These are necessary aspects of writing, and the chances are you will be thinking or researching outside your allotted hours anyway.

It can help you see where you are going if you decide how long you can write for each week, and set a deadline for your first project. Then keep records of the time set aside to write and what is achieved, what research you have done, notes made, and how many words or pages you have done in draft or revised.

How much historical knowledge do you need?

To write a historical novel successfully I believe you need to have a reasonable background knowledge of the period about which you intend to write.

If, let's say, you want to write about the time of Queen Elizabeth the First, it is necessary to know something about the Tudors and some previous history indicating how and why they acquired the throne.

Without this it might be impossible to understand the conflicts of the time, how people felt and why they behaved as they did. You need to understand England's relations with the rest of Europe, the religious tensions in England and elsewhere in Europe, and something about everyday life.

Dates can be looked up and minor details can be researched, but without a good general background knowledge you will be inclined to make mistakes or not research something which ought to be researched because you don't see the necessity.

Write what you know

This does not mean you have to have every last detail at your fingertips. You can research them. But choose a time about which you know quite a lot and preferably one you like. 'Write what you know' is advice frequently given to writers, but we cannot know, in person, what life was like centuries ago. We have to find out through research.

Prepare to research

There are, I find when writing my own novels, three stages of research: the overall situation, what's going on in the country and the world, and such things as the attitudes to women, religious and social background, technological and medical knowledge. It helps to have a fair amount of knowledge about these things before you start.

Then, narrowing this down to a specific time, a year and month, and a location, you need to know what is happening then, specific national and local events.

Finally, there are the tiny details that crop up during the writing of the book. For instance, for my book *Lord Hugo's Wedding*, I had to find out whether my hero and heroine could marry in France during the seventeenth century, and what the formalities were.

Imagination is important too

If you write historical novels or fantasy it must by its very nature be about something you have not experienced. Crime novelists are not all murderers or detectives. Imagination and research are essential in all forms of writing, to add to, flesh out or make bare facts interesting.

Be aware of special problems

As you are doing your research, don't depend on one source. This applies especially to the Internet, where anyone is free to put up anything they like, which may not be accurate. Consult two authorities and, if they disagree, a third. Don't rely on other novels for facts, either – even the most meticulous novelists may get some things wrong.

It is always the small detail we think we know, or don't think necessary to check, that traps us. These can be things such as the materials used in clothing, or the customs of the time such as addressing people by surname, or wearing hats indoors.

Know the industry

If you were planning to open a restaurant you would look at the competition and decide where a good location would give you the best chance of success. Writing is similar. Look and see what is popular, whether the market seems overcrowded, new trends and, if at all possible, a gap in the market which fits in with the popular image.

Steer a course between innovation and imitation. Editors say they want something new, but cannot say what, only that they will recognise it when they see it. On the other hand, something too different could fail because publishers cannot see a way of marketing it within their existing framework.

Study the market

Many excellent pieces of writing fail to find publishers. Rejections are often based on considerations quite apart from the quality of the writing. Perhaps the publisher has just bought a book similar in some way, has no room for a new one or has already spent the budget.

The writer may have sent it to the wrong place or at the wrong time or been unlucky because a publisher liked but could not use it. It pays to find out about publishers and to meet authors. You can read the trade journals *The Bookseller* and *Publisher's News* in libraries. Go to talks by authors and agents.

Historical Novel Society Review

The HNS publishes a quarterly magazine containing reviews of most of the historical novels published in the UK during that quarter and many published in other English-speaking countries. This is an excellent source for finding out what sort of novels are being published now. They also have a twice-yearly magazine, *Solander*, with author interviews and informative articles.

Do you need help or encouragement?

Writers differ. Some prefer to be on their own, to finish what they are writing and only then show it to anyone else. Others like to have the opinions of others as they go.

How to find support

This can be from relatives, or local, national, indeed international groups. However, be cautious of praise from friends and relatives. They will probably be astonished that you have written a complete novel and they won't wish to hurt you by adverse criticism, but they are unlikely to be judges of what is wanted by the publishers. You need help which is of practical value.

Networking

Talking and just being with others in the same profession, who know the problems and can often provide the solutions to them, inspires ideas and confidence. It also provides tips on markets. Getting to know other writers can give you valuable contacts.

Groups

You could join a local or national group, or a creative writing class. You might attend day, weekend or longer courses. You could take a correspondence course. You do not have to be alone.

Local groups meet in homes or public halls, libraries and local papers will have details. Some cater for all interests or just one, such as poetry.

Most have evenings of reading and discussing manuscripts. These can be useful for receiving the opinions of others and meeting fellow writers to discuss common problems. Groups sometimes have outside speakers – editors, agents or other writers, which is a good opportunity to ask questions and begin to network. Try a couple of meetings first. Make sure you have the same objectives as the rest of the group.

National organisations

Many published writers belong to the Society of Authors. The Crime Writers' Association admits only published crime writers. The Romantic Novelists' Association has a scheme for giving critiques to unpublished new writers. The British Fantasy Society is open to non-writers. Historical novelists can join the HNS. Details of others are in the yearbooks.

Creative writing classes

These are usually run by the Local Education Authority. Libraries have details. They can be for the beginner or a continuing course where people attend for several years, and can even be university and post-graduate level.

Some may be for particular areas of writing, but most are general. Try to sample a class before spending time and money and, if you aim to be published, ensure that the tutor has up-to-date knowledge of the commercial prospects.

Courses, conferences and festivals

Day schools, weekend or week-long courses and conferences can be fun and provide opportunities to meet top people. They can be talks or workshops and are advertised in magazines for writers. Many are for specific types of writing, so you can choose one to fit in with your own interests.

There are also festivals with numerous activities going on at the same time. There could be lectures, courses and lots of opportunities for congenial shop talk. At literary festivals you can listen to and meet writers.

The value of listening to practising writers is hearing how they work, picking up hints and seeing different ways to do things.

Distance learning

Correspondence courses are valuable for people who cannot attend classes or who wish to work at their own pace. They are usually specific to one kind of writing and you will get personal tuition but at a distance. Good courses are organised so that you can be doing the next lesson while awaiting the return of the last.

Choose colleges recognised by a professional body such as The Council for the Accreditation of Correspondence Colleges. Make sure you choose a course where you can pay as you go in case it is not suitable for your needs.

The Internet

There are now many on-line courses, some run chat room style, others with individual feedback. Some groups, normally just a few people, swap their work for mutual appraisal. Others, which can be a larger group, exist mainly to chat about their work or the industry.

Questions to answer and things to do

These can all be done alongside your writing. Don't be distracted by doing them instead of getting down to the actual process of writing your novel! You can do both.

1. Prepare systems for keeping your notes, e.g. cards, notebooks, folders. Notebooks are fine for making notes as you go, either from visits to libraries or museums, but it could be difficult to find the details afterwards. File cards are more accessible, and you can sort them and even write them up while you are doing the research.

   Many people like to keep their notes on a computer, and in these days of laptop and handheld machines it is possible to take them with you on trips and type in the information there and then. There are also small portable scanners, rather like pens, which you can use to scan a line at a time, which saves writing out notes from books.

   Be cautious about using these aids, however. Some libraries may not allow it if their documents and books are old and fragile. And there is always the temptation to reproduce the actual words you have copied instead of putting the facts into your own words and style.

2. Check your reference books to see if there are gaps you want to fill.

   A good dictionary is a must. You might also find a spelling dictionary (without the definitions) is easier to handle than the larger sort. Computers have online spellcheckers and definitions, but watch what language is being used. Some are American English, for example, which is not helpful to the British author. They are not comprehensive and spellcheckers cannot differentiate between the meanings of correctly spelled words. If you type 'pot' when you mean 'lot', the spellchecker won't highlight or correct it.

   A historical atlas might be useful if your books are to be set in specific places. A book of dates which gives the main political, cultural, scientific and technical events year by year helps you to focus on what is happening outside the narrow confines of your story and slip in allusions to current events.

   Books on food, houses and costume will supply some of the small, telling details which enhance novels, whilst a biographical dictionary will give you the main outline of a life and sources for more detailed accounts.

Whatever your special interests, you will begin to collect books of general histories of the time, biographies of people who lived then and, if at all possible, diaries written at the time.

Books of names, such as *Brewer's Dictionary of Names*, list names popular at various times and in different countries.

It is essential to have a current Yearbook once you are ready to send the novel to an agent or publisher. They have lists of both and what they prefer to have sent, for example, just a synopsis or the first few chapters. There are also details of organisations and courses, competitions and useful articles on such matters as taxation.

3. Start a file for useful Internet websites.

A majority of the UK population now has access to the Internet, but if you don't you can use computers in libraries and Internet cafés. This makes it possible to find all sorts of information.

To begin with use one of the search engines such as Google, Yahoo or Dogpile, and when you find a site that has useful information you might want in future, bookmark it. It could also be valuable to make a note of what in particular the site offers.

4. Start a list of publishers who take historicals.

You will probably concentrate first on those in your own country, but be aware of others in English-speaking countries. The sales will be greater in the USA, but your style and subject matter may appeal more to English publishers.

Use the HNS *Review* and then look up the publishers in one of the yearbooks. What do they appear to prefer or specialise in? Try to look on their websites where some of them have guidelines, or their catalogues with brief descriptions of the books they are publishing.

5. Study the sort of historicals being published now, and visit bookshops to see them on the shelf.

Reading current novels is essential. Although older novels can teach us some skills, it is a waste of time to attempt to write in the fashion or style of people published a hundred, twenty or even five years ago, because fashions change and so do the requirements of publishers and readers. This includes such things as total length, style and length of individual scenes, amount of description and pace.

6. Look at magazines and organisations that might be of use.

   As well as the HNS magazines *Solander* and the *Review*, look at some of the popular magazines devoted to one or more aspects of history, for example History *Today*, *Medieval History*, or family history magazines such as *Family History Monthly*, *Family Tree* or *Practical Family History*.

   In recent issues I came across articles on child labour in the factories, murder in ancient Greece and Rome, nineteenth-century women doctors and medieval prostitution, all of which gave me ideas for themes, plots and incidents or sources for further research.

7. Start collecting details of people of the time, places and events which might help your research.

   This is assuming you have a period and place in mind, so you can look for photographs, maps and town plans. Visit if you can, get maps of the time, pictures, contemporary accounts and portraits.

8. Keep a writing diary of when you have been writing and adjust your targets if they are not realistic.

   Don't forget, time spent researching also counts towards this target time, but try to get into the habit of doing some writing every day or every few days because it is a very real temptation to be so absorbed in the research you don't get on with the writing.

9. Are you an expert in something, such as the history of transport, or weapons?

   If you are, try to capitalise on special knowledge or even acquire it and make yourself an expert. Readers tend to like this. It can be local knowledge of an area or industry, or more general knowledge of, say, horse transport or weaponry.

10. Make a list of historical themes appropriate to different times.

Depending on the period, certain themes will be treated differently in different centuries. For instance, until comparatively recently slavery was accepted and your eighteenth-century family in the deep south of America might well have owned a plantation worked by slaves. In the nineteenth century there would have been deep divisions and conflict caused by this. In the twentieth century slavery was condemned.

Religious wars or arguments could have formed the theme of adventure novels in many past times but today religious disputes tend to be treated as serious topics, not fictional entertainment.

11. Do you read biographies and history books?

It helps if you do, for pleasure as well as research, because there are so many tiny facts you absorb while doing this background reading. They will influence the atmosphere of your books, that indefinable something which adds to the reality.

12. Have you done any research in archives, with original sources?

Most historical novelists use secondary sources, published books about their period, but there is much available in local history and other specialist libraries and museums which can give you useful background. For example, for my saga *The Golden Road*, I read the contemporary motoring magazines to find out about the Monte Carlo Rally and went to a meeting where I could look at the cars built during the time my characters were driving them.

There are lots of records such as judicial reports, school log books and local newspapers, which are readily available.

The many re-enactment societies can also be a valuable source of authentic detail. Visit their events and living history museums where you may be able to talk to experts. I have found the Black Country Museum and museums of reconstructed buildings, such as the Chilterns Museum, fascinating as well as full of facts. There are knowledgeable guides who can answer many questions.

13. Have you done any family history research?

This is a very popular pastime and if you have done any it can often help with small details, such as the occasional comments in church registers about what was happening – even the weather. Census returns can show occupations, sizes and composition of families. Don't ignore these sources if you need such small details.

14. Take your idea of a novel from Chapter I and make a list of things you may have to research.

Tips by example

For my examples I would do the following:

1. Pepys – read a biography, read at least some sections of the diary, find out about 1660s London, get maps of the time, read biographies of other people important at the time and books on the costume and social life.

2. Read books about the 1950s – look at contemporary newspapers. Decide on a location, a setting, and collect photographs, maps and guidebooks about it from that period or as near to it as possible.

Key points

1. There is no one ideal method of working. Find the best for you.

2. Start collecting useful books.

3. Set up an efficient working space and keep it to yourself.

4. Learn about the publishing world.

5. Decide if you need support or help.

Getting started

Characters or plot?

The question is often asked, which comes first, plot or characters? The answer is either or neither. They are interdependent. You need an idea for lift-off, and this can be a plot, a character, a setting, an incident, a theme, a title or a few words. We will look at all these in more detail in later chapters. Here we have an overview, and start on the actual writing.

Make characters appropriate

Characters must be appropriate for your novel. As a very simple example, if you choose to write about wartime you will have soldiers or sailors and, in the twentieth century, airmen. A book set in England before the Reformation is more likely to have monks and nuns than one set after the dissolution of the monasteries.

Characters can provide ideas for the plot, for incidents and twists, and the way in which they behave, in whatever situation you place them, can well influence the development of the plot.

Your characters are actors and if you can see them this way, as if in scenes on a stage, it brings them alive for you and therefore helps you to make them real for your readers. Visualise the action as it takes place. Most writers find this works.

Deciding how many

Create as few as possible. P. G. Wodehouse said one big one was worth two small ones. Some will be essential in order to do certain things, and these vary from the main characters to the servants or hotel receptionists who have to be there in the background.

Don't forget that people have family, friends, neighbours and colleagues. They provide your main characters with a background, a history, with all the relationships and complications involved, even if they don't feature directly in the story.

Other minor characters round out the lives or demonstrate character traits of the main characters, even if off-stage. This could be a bedridden old lady the heroine visits, which can show her compassion or helpfulness.

Theme, story and plot

They are not the same, though we do tend to use the words story and plot interchangeably.

Theme

Theme is the impulse behind the plot. It's often an abstract notion like jealousy, revenge or ambition. It can be more concrete such as a search, a conflict or coping with change. We will look at some in Chapter 6 on Plotting. Themes can provide ideas.

Story

A story is not necessarily a plot. A story can be a series of events, rather like diary entries. A plot is more.

E. M. Forster illustrates this with a simple example: 'The king dies. The queen dies.' This is a story, a relation of a succession of unrelated events. If you add 'The queen died of grief,' you have linked the two events – one is a result of the other, the first causes the second. This is a plot, with a causal relationship.

Plot

A plot is a series of cause and effect events told in a dramatic way. The actions described have consequences. As the author, you are in control in that you are deciding which events are important and showing them in a particular way.

Be original

You need to be original. The events you are relating must be strong, realistic and believable, but above all different and original.

Don't worry if you cannot find a plot which seems original. It's been said there are only so many plots, though the precise number varies between seven, twenty or however many various writers choose to list. Ronald A. Tobias has written an excellent book, *Twenty Master Plots*, in which he analyses the different types of plots under headings such as Adventure, Quest, Transformation. This book is illuminating and will certainly stimulate ideas.

How can you be original within this restriction?

It's the treatment that matters. Plots are like a child's building blocks – the same limited variety of shapes and colours which can be built up into hundreds of different combinations. If you gave ten people the same basic idea, situation and set of characters you would finish up with ten different plots.

Be believable

You need to be believable. Even in fantasy you need to make readers suspend disbelief, to catch their imagination somehow, with that combination of character and narrative that makes them care what happens to the characters even though they know it is fiction.

Readers know it's unreal, but for the time they are reading they want to believe, and it's up to you to convince them by making your characters real, the plots logical and the resolutions of crises apparently inevitable. Don't make your characters do impossible things, and remember it's lazy plotting and breaks your implied contract with the reader to get out of difficulties with unforeseeable coincidences, or bringing on the *deus ex machina*, the god from the machine, who arrives to sort out the mess made by mere mortals.

Where do you get ideas?

Writers have said their ideas come from words overheard in a bus queue, places, people, settings, observing people, a news item or personal experiences. You may decide to have certain backgrounds in your books, such as the theatre or gardens or houses. Until you get into the habit of it, it may be difficult to know where to look for ideas.

You may have too few ideas because you are not yet used to recognising them for what they are or might be. These can be for characters or incidents or complete novels. Turning phrases, people or situations into plots is an important way in which writers differ from other people.

Looking for ideas

If you are stuck for ideas, don't rely on inspiration as you look out of your window. It's unlikely to work. Check through the following list and jot down notes. You are sure to come up with several potential ideas, if not for complete novels, for incidents or backgrounds.

People you know, see or read about

As historical novelists you have the entire range of people from the past. But present-day people can also give you ideas. Take some well-known person, a politician or actor, and think what they could have been like a couple of centuries ago. Give them a different profession. Maybe the politician was a parson or the actor someone on the fringes of society desperate to be accepted and overdoing his attempts to be noticed.

A Cabinet Minister today, from a humble family, would not have been able to enter Parliament at all in the eighteenth or nineteenth centuries. How might he have behaved, if he had had strong convictions? He could have been a revolutionary, a Luddite, Chartist or trade unionist. A woman would probably have been a suffragette.

Places you know, go to or read about

The idea for one of my novels, *Sybilla and the Privateer*, sprang partly from a holiday in the Loire Valley and Brittany and incidents I read about in guide books.

Major events such as war, terrorism, earthquakes

Think of the many novels set against the backdrop of the twentieth-century World Wars. Some authors may use the events in great detail, others very lightly.

Historical events

I have taken battles and sieges of the English Civil War and constructed novels around them, involving my characters in the real events but also giving them concerns and problems apart from this.

Individual triumphs and tragedies

Reading about individuals, real biographies or diaries can give you ideas for characters in similar situations. A nurse in the Crimea, an English governess in Russia, a Scottish emigrant to Canada after the Highland Clearances can start you thinking of how your own characters, those you have created, might be in similar situations.

Phrases overheard

'The fire raged for days' might start you thinking of the Great Fire of London or what would happen to the owners and neighbours of any house or business which burned down.

Diaries

We already have Pepys as one of the examples being used here as the basis for a novel about a real person but there are lots of diaries and books of reminiscences. You don't need to use all the events or write about that person, but you might create a similar character or use some of the events described for your own book.

I have drawn on many books of reminiscences written about Birmingham in the first half of the twentieth century for details of what life was like then, and ideas for the situations the characters in my Midlands sagas might encounter.

Advertisements

A simple job advertisement, say for an office clerk or a housekeeper, especially if it states the wages offered or the conditions, might make you wonder what that person's life could be like.

Agony columns

These cover such a huge range of human problems that they are fertile sources of ideas. Many of them relate to life today, but see if you can move them back in time. What about the young men who don't know how to meet young women? How would they be likely to set about it in 1900? Or 1700?

Newspaper and magazine letter columns

Often these are letters of complaint, about the government or other public servants. In magazines they often tell amusing stories. How could the complainer, if you take him back a few centuries, deal with the problem? Can you expand the amusing incident into something bigger? Can you put two or more items together to get some sort of connection?

Guide books

When these tell you about the history of a town or a castle you could put your own characters there, use the physical background and some of the historical events.

Art books and paintings

These will show possible locations, houses, interiors, antiques, people and costumes.

Photographs

These are available in vast numbers and, if you look for those published in small books showing how a particular town used to look, you will see they show far more than just the buildings. They will show how much traffic was around, what sort, what the people were wearing, shop fronts, advertisements on hoardings or buildings.

Myths, legends and fairy stories

Adapt them to a different time. Use the idea of the tortoise and the hare in some other competitive situation, such as rival woollen mill owners anxious to use newly invented machinery. Change Dick Whittington and suppose he turned back and didn't get to London?

Titles, first lines and quotations

Just think how many book titles are taken from quotations. Have you ever wondered whether the author found the title first and made up a story around it? Take a famous title, such as *Three Men in a Boat*, and devise a new story to fit. It could be a shipwreck, smugglers or fishermen.

Coffee table books

These can often give you details of houses, furnishings and gardens, all sorts of things which, even if they don't provide an idea for a whole novel, could provide ideas for details or locations.

Using ideas

Many writers say they have far more ideas than they can ever use. Sometimes the problem is knowing which make viable stories: which are sensible, big enough to hang a complete novel on or at least something to build on, to make a complete novel. You only need one to keep on working. It's the way you use ideas that's important.

Dealing with ideas

Ideas emerge from the subconscious, based on things we encounter. We then treat them consciously by bombarding them with information, playing with alternative possibilities, planning how to use them and what we need to research about them.

Turning vague ideas into plots is a skill possessed by novelists. Other people may see the same things, hear the same words, but they don't see the fictional possibilities. You have had an idea, done some research, made lots of notes, and then perhaps you can't see the way forward or impose any sort of order on your creation. Don't worry. This is a normal part of the creative process.

If you are really stuck there are Internet sites and programs which offer help with developing plots, but I feel that a writer's own imagination will produce fresher ideas rather than mechanical answers.

Ideas can be left to germinate

If you feel you have a mass of unrelated ideas that will never combine into a usable plot, sleep on them. The subconscious will get to work for you. The mass of ideas will begin to take on a shape, form patterns and you will have the basis of a plot. The important ideas and facts will float to the surface, begging to be used.

Trust your instinct and work on these. Your novel will start to become more real, a concrete idea instead of a hazy soup of unconnected snippets. It is probably at this point that you will need to do more specific research.

Ask questions

Whenever you see, hear or read something which might be the germ of an idea, ask questions.

- Who (are these people, could they be characters in your book and, if it's a house, who lived there)?
- What (are they, do they do, is their nature)?
- How (did it happen, did it get there, could it change)?
- When (did it happen, did they meet, did they part)?
- Why (does it exist, did it happen then, there, and to them)?
- Where (did it happen, and why there, and how)?
- What if (any number of possibilities occur)?

Suppose you see a small castle or fortified manor house, apply the above questions to the people who might have lived in it at various times.

An example

Imagine an English village of the 1920s with several houses around the green and in the High Street. What are they? Let's suppose a vicarage, a bank, a grocer, butcher, baker, chemist, a pub, a dress shop, a small tea room, a garage with a petrol pump, a blacksmith's forge, houses belonging to a rich farmer, a retired businessman, the widow of a former rector, the schoolmaster, and cottages of farm labourers.

Who lives in each? There will be families, babies and older children, elderly relatives, live-in maids in the larger houses, maybe a housekeeper or two, or nannies, and they will have relatives and other visitors.

What jobs do they do? Don't confine your imagination to the householder, but consider the rest of the family or any lodgers. Do they have hobbies or passionate interests or obsessions?

Given this wide selection of people, what are their backgrounds? Have they lived here long? What liaisons or quarrels might they have, amongst each other or outside?

What event, such as a newcomer arriving or a sudden tragedy, might spark off a whole series of consequences?

If you haven't gleaned several ideas for plots and situations, go back and ask further questions or devise different answers.

Keeping track of ideas

Make notes! Write ideas down and file them. You will soon have far more than you will ever use, but just browsing through them can start the creative process off again.

Choosing the right title

This doesn't have to be chosen first, but often titles come during the planning stage. Consider possibilities now, since a title often expresses the main theme of the novel.

Sometimes titles only come when the book is finished. A phrase or incident or character in the novel can suggest one. Don't worry if you can't think of the ideal title now, but work hard to find a good one before you send your manuscript out.

They are important

Some editors say a good title helps catch their attention.

A sparkling or intriguing title helps to sell a book, in the first instance to an editor if it shows your originality and writing talent, and later to the reader who might be attracted by it. But titles can be changed and frequently are. Publishers may have their own preferences or they may have published a book with a similar title and don't want to confuse readers. Some people say that titles might put them off reading a book. You want to entice them into it.

They must be appropriate

Titles can inform and intrigue. Especially with historicals they can indicate to the reader the time at which the book is set or the type of book. I used *Restoration Affair* for one of my early books set in the 1660s, and *Strife Beyond Tamar* for another based around the Civil War fighting in Cornwall. One of my Regencies was called *Petronella's Waterloo*, which showed the time and the location, since I had my heroine travelling to Brussels at the time of the battle.

The narrative hook

After the title, the first few sentences have to draw the reader into the story. Don't forget editors are your first readers – they have to be persuaded to read on. Ask yourself, is the opening page arresting? Have you started with something important, probably at some turning point in the character's life, with some event which is of vital importance to your protagonists?

Make it active

The most effective beginning is to get right into the action. Of course, it is possible to begin with a description, perhaps of a setting or character, but this can be rather static and is less easy to do. The danger is that the reader will become bored. Be wary of this until you have had a good deal of practice.

Action involves a scene with characters. They are doing something, preferably caught in the middle of it. It's boring to begin with a lot of build-up and explanation. If possible make this action just before a major event or confrontation. You can always insert the necessary background information later on, explain who they are and what is happening. If you have enticed readers to turn over the first page in order to find this out, you are half way to persuading them to read the whole book.

In *The Cobweb Cage* there is anticipation and fear.

Marigold squatted on the edge of the fender, huddled as close as she dared to the banked-up fire. Despite the heat from the coals, which warmed her face and chest, and her thick flannel nightgown, she shivered uncontrollably. Twisting round to warm her back, she clutched her thin arms about her body in a vain attempt to dispel the bewildered emptiness within her.

When would Johnny come home? What would Pa say if he came home to find the table still littered with dirty plates, and no dinner cooked?

At this thought she shook still more. Pa loved them. He wasn't cruel, not like Mr Potter next door, who took off his belt to thrash Fred and Tom and little Betty for the slightest offence...

Indicate conflict

This can be of a personal nature, such as in the example above, or a more general one facing a particular group of people.

Readers' views

Many readers have told me how important they consider the first page and paragraph, they want to have their interest engaged right away and to get into the story quickly. The book will probably be read if the first page grabs their attention.

The functions of the first few pages are many

Because you have to do so many things in these first few paragraphs, take great care over them. Many writers only do a rough draft to begin with, and then, when they have finished the book, go back to rewrite and polish this crucial opening.

Show the type of book

As we have shown above, you need to attract the reader's interest. It helps to do this if you can indicate the type of book and show the mood and style of the writing, so that the reader knows they will feel comfortable with it and that something good is coming.

Bring on a main character

The most important thing is to introduce one of the main characters, and perhaps one or two others. Readers like to follow the fortunes of someone and they tend to prefer the first character they meet. If this turns out not to be a main character they can feel cheated and they may find it difficult to switch their identification to another character.

We talk of having sympathy or empathy with characters. Having sympathy with a character is not a question of feeling sorry for them but of caring what happens to them, being able to share their emotions and experiences even if we would not necessarily like them or approve of their actions in real life.

The opening of *The Glowing Hours* contrasts the character of Nell with those of her brothers and sisters. She is more adventurous than they are, and both angry at their fear yet understanding it.

> *'Ain't none on yer comin'?'*
>
> *Nell, poised astride the narrow windowsill, stuffed her ragged petticoat into the red flannel bloomers. She looked over her shoulder. Nine pairs of eyes, some envious, most apprehensive, stared back at her. How defeated they looked, she thought with a spurt of irritation. They were so passive, so unwilling to fight. Little red-haired Amy was the only one ever to show a scrap of spirit, and she'd soon have it beaten out of her. Then she was ashamed of her scorn. They hadn't had any chance to experience a different sort of life.*

In *The Golden Road* we have another character who is showing different characteristics. Josie is angry at the guests because they do not appear to be as sorry as she is for the death of her stepfather.

> *Josie Shaw, feeling desperately large and awkward in her new black clothes, stood dutifully beside her diminutive mother and scowled at the assembled mourners. How could they look so cheerful, even laugh out loud, when they had just attended the burial of her stepfather, one of the kindest, most generous of men? Even her mother had thrown back the ostentatiously heavy veils she had worn at the church over her fair hair, and though she clutched a black lace handkerchief in her hand, her eyes were dry and she was talking volubly.*
>
> *Josie glared round. She wished they would all go away.*

Establish the time and place

In a historical, it is more important than for contemporary books to establish the time and place as soon as possible. There are many ways of doing this. The title may help. My first book's title was *Cavalier Courtship*, which indicated the time as well as the genre, a romantic novel.

One of the simplest methods is to put the date and place as a chapter heading, but there are less direct ways of conveying the information. And sometimes just hinting can flatter the reader who feels pleased to have guessed correctly.

There are many ways of indicating the date, less precisely, but sufficiently clearly so that most readers will at least know which century they are in. You could mention a well-known event such as the death of a monarch or a famous battle, something that the reader is likely to have heard about, and have at least a rough idea of when this happened.

You can be more precise later on, if this is necessary, by finding a way of mentioning the date or one close to it in the text. This could be that someone was born twenty years ago, in 1750.

You will soon think of other ways of getting in this information fairly early on, even if not right at the start. You could mention clothing such as the farthingale or crinoline, or refer to new-fangled inventions such as the railways, motor cars or the wireless. Use the terms common then, not the more usual car or radio we would use today. These hints would, with most readers who have a smattering of historical knowledge, establish the right decade.

The place, the town and country can be established indirectly too. If you have people driving in Hyde Park, most people would know this is in London. Mention of the Prince Regent's Pavilion would place the setting in Brighton.

Don't confuse the readers

If you are introduced to a dozen people at once, can you remember all their names? Start with one or two main characters, but avoid bringing in too many to begin with or the reader will be confused. They need time to absorb what to them is new information.

Each character they meet needs to have something that readers will remember and associate with them. This can be a physical characteristic, such as vivid red hair or a broken nose, but sometimes an attitude can make a bigger impression. If the character is clearly furious, vindictive or timid, readers will remember. And readers develop an attitude towards all characters by how they first meet them, so make these introductions appropriate, emphasising the things you want your reader to feel – pity, amusement, liking or loathing.

Prepare for what follows

It isn't necessary to explain everything at the start. If you pose sufficiently intriguing questions the reader will want to continue in order to find the answers.

In *Forbidden Love*, the opening suggests various possibilities and the reader wants to discover whether they are as it seems, and how they move on.

They were in the church, a small, ill-lit place where the tombs of the dead overawed the living, before Bella awoke from the daze that had held her unresisting for the past two days. She shook her head slightly to clear her mind as they left the chill sunlight of the early April day and entered the dank cold of the stone building. Her companion, interpreting the gesture as a refusal, tightened his grip on her arm and hustled her onwards.

'Oh no, you don't! It's too late now to draw back. You made your choice and must abide by it. Edward is waiting for you, and an anxious bridegroom he is.'

Who is this? Is this a forced marriage? If so, why? Why had Bella been in a daze? Had she been drugged? There are lots of questions and the reader will read on to find the answers.

Make it dramatic

If you start with a dramatic event, make sure you can follow it with something better. If it's the most dramatic event in the story the rest is a let-down. Novels need variations, ups and downs in the level of intensity, but the main crisis should be as near the end as possible.

Come back to it

If your beginning isn't right, don't get bogged down. A frequent reason for not completing a novel is that the would-be writer spends all his time perfecting the beginning and never gets past chapter one.

Carry on, write the rest of the book, and come back to the beginning later. Many authors do it last of all, since often a later incident can suggest the ideal opening. And you may find that information you tried to include in the first few pages fits more naturally later on.

If you have a few moments to spare, you can practise writing good openings. It doesn't have to be a real novel you are working on at the moment, but develop ideas as they come, and file them for future possible use.

Beware of too much back history

This is a common fault with inexperienced writers. Having introduced a character or two they feel compelled to explain everything about the former history, character, and motivations of these people. Don't!

Dropping out of the drama, often for a whole chapter, even for a couple of paragraphs, completely destroys the impetus of the story. It slows the pace and frequently bores the reader so much they give up. Readers cannot absorb a lot of detailed information all at once, and until they have some sort of feeling for the character they are reading about, they are not really interested. Also, in these explanations, writers tend to give a lot of unnecessary information.

There are ways of including the essential information later on, as and when it becomes important or necessary to understand a character's behaviour. You could mention, when the occasion arises, that a heroine's fear of dogs was because she was once bitten by one. This could be done by the heroine or someone else who would know saying it, or the heroine thinking it, or another character making some comment and the explanation being given in reply.

If necessary, though this is less advisable and I will be looking at why later on, you could drop into a brief flashback.

Questions to answer and things to do

1. Jot down a few appropriate titles for your novel.

   From my examples we could have *Peep into Pepys*, which is terribly corny but might fit a comic novel. At this stage any idea is worth noting, as it may well lead on to other more suitable titles. *And So To Bed* is the well-known phrase connected to the diary, and many people would recognise it, but it has been used so many times it is rather a cliché.

   For the second example *Post-War Blues* is a plain, straightforward descriptive title. As the novel progresses, an idea for a better or more appropriate title might come to you.

   Ideas for titles come in all sorts of ways. I once lived in a house called Half Hidden, and Emma Blair commented that it was a wonderful title. When I had not used it several years later, Emma Blair did for one of her novels.

2. Write an opening paragraph and make it as enticing as you can.

The following, which could be the start for the first of my two examples, shows what sort of things to include.

Samuel Pepys threw down the quill, scattered sand over the manuscript, and stretched his aching fingers. Another day's events recorded. It was hard to keep up this diary, after a busy day at the naval office, but it gave him considerable satisfaction and relieved his frustrations to put down his real thoughts, in the knowledge that no one else could pry into his secret language.

'Samuel?' It was his wife Elizabeth calling, and he smiled and stood up.

Especially he didn't want Elizabeth to read his thoughts about their maidservants. A man had to have his little pleasures. He smiled again. Bedtime, and Elizabeth was still young and eager.

I have posed various questions, such as which is the day referred to, why he was frustrated, and a hint of his behaviour towards the maidservants.

I have also included contemporary details of quill and sand. How to insert details naturally is something we will be looking at later.

3. Draft an outline of your plot, in as much or as little detail as you think you need.

For my second example, as I usually start with just a very vague outline, this is the sort of thing I might do. I will deal with just one character, but would devise similar brief outlines for the other two girls.

Marion's father, newly rich, wants her to stay at home, go to lots of social events and meet a wealthy young man. She is determined to resist this, so insists on getting a job and training as a nurse. Her choice is partly because she feels guilty about the way her father made his money during the war, and she thinks she can make up for it to some extent by helping others. She hates the reality of the wards, but struggles on out of pride and reluctance to admit her mistake. There are two men in her life, a doctor her family approve of, but who is rather overbearing, like her father and an injured soldier from a poor background who has ideas for inventing better and more effective guns. Hating the war, she cannot accept this.

There is sufficient conflict here, with her dislike of the job, the relationships with her parents and the two men, to provide lots of action.

4. Make a timeline for the real events that happen during the course of your novel.

The following example is from the 1660s, choosing only a few varied events, and it could look something like this:

Date	National evens	International events
1660	Charles II restored to throne	Louis XIV marries maria Theresa Charles X of Sweden dies
1661	Lambert executed	Louis XIV assumes absolute power
1662	Charles marries Catherine of Braganza	Royal Society founded
1663	First Turnpike Act	Colony of North Carolina estalished
1664	Second Dutch war starts	English capture New Amsterdam, renamed New York

5. How many of these real events do you intend to incorporate into the fictional plot?

Beware of too many if your main characters are fictional. Don't distract attention and turn it into a history book.

6. Start a file of ideas you may use in the future.

Inevitably, as you research or as you write, you will think of other plots, other good characters, incidents which don't fit here but might in another book.

7. As you write, keep a list of scenes, the time they happen, and the main characters in each.

Tips by example

From my second suggested plot:

1946		
June	Marion and father	They disagree about her wanting a job
June	Marion and Peggy	At school Marion talks about the row, and Peggy says she's lucky to have a father
June	Jennifer and Head	Jennifer explains she has to get a job, cannot stay on at school or go to university
June	Peggy	Has telegram at home, afraid, but not about her father
July	Marion and mother	Tries to explain feelings to unsympathetic mother
July	Jennifer	She is looking for a job in the town where they live

Key points

1. Theme, story and plot are different.
2. Ideas can be found in many places.
3. Using ideas creatively, asking questions.
4. Finding the right title.
5. The narrative hook.
6. The first few pages are vital.
7. Introduce the main characters first.
8. Establish the time and place.
9. Avoid back history.

Characters 1 – people are same the world over

Choose your cast carefully

Your characters are like actors in a drama. If you see them this way, in scenes on a stage, it helps to bring them alive for you and therefore helps you to make them real for your readers. Imagine the action as it takes place. Most writers find this works, especially those who may also write scripts for films and TV.

Characters must be right for your novel. They can provide ideas for the plot, for incidents and twists, and often the plot arises out of your characters – if you have drawn them well you will know what their reactions might be in any given situation.

Who do you need?

Create as few as possible, but try to have the main characters invented before you begin to plot. Small ones can be added later for specific purposes if there is not an existing character who can perform that function.

The scale of importance varies. In category romances very few characters appear apart from the hero and heroine. In most crime novels several characters have to be of similar importance to provide a believable list of suspects.

Differing importance

The protagonists are the most important characters, at the top of your list. There are usually two, occasionally three – the good guys. These can be the hero and heroine, the sleuths, the army commanders. There may also be an antagonist, the bad guys, for example a rival, a villain or the enemy commander. Depending on the scope of your novel there will be a few or several biggish ones who are on-stage a lot, powerful enough to influence events and about whom readers care. Caring is not liking. Readers care about a character when they want him to receive his just deserts, be this reward or punishment. If readers are indifferent to a major character the writer has not succeeded.

Then there will be some minor characters who play small but important, necessary parts, but don't have to appear very much.

Finally there are what in the theatre are called the extras or walk-ons like postillions and footmen who are essential in the tasks they perform but are only scenery.

It always helps to analyse published books. Take one you know quite well and list all the characters in order of importance, label the protagonists, major, minor and walk-ons. Ask whether any of them could be dispensed with totally or their role be given to another character? Then do the same with your own casts of characters.

Have a variety

In most plots you need people of different sexes, ages, appearances, occupations and dispositions. This makes the situation more natural and interesting. Identify them as far as possible by giving them individual voices, that is, particular turns of speech, or favourite words or phrases.

Readers often like to read about people from similar groups to their own but they also want characters to be intriguing, different from themselves. They will find more variety in historicals.

In some stories characters need someone in whom they can confide or with whom they can discuss or share information. Most detectives have a sidekick, most romantic heroines a best friend. Make these characters interesting in themselves, active in the story. Give them other functions, apart from being just a confidante.

Getting to know them

Many writers, though not all, compile lists of their characters' physical and other attributes before they start. These are character profiles, and it often helps to do them, particularly if you are wondering where to start.

One device often used is to cut out pictures of interesting-looking people and pin them up on a board so that you can see what your characters are like. I have an entire folder of pictures taken from magazines and newspapers and when I start a new novel I select likely looking pictures for each of my characters. Beside the pictures I can keep notes on the profile I have drawn up for each main character.

It's probably a little more difficult to find pictures of historical characters in the dress of the time, but you could photocopy them from books, or just use heads and draw on appropriate hair styles, bonnets, wigs and so on.

It helps you to remember what characters look like, but a good profile also shows how they might react to various situations. They are notes for guidance, however, and are not necessarily used in the book. As the book progresses, other attributes are likely to be added to the basic list as you get to know your characters more intimately.

A sample character profile

These are the sorts of things you might jot down about your protagonists and major characters. Can you think of other questions?

Look at their family background, the real basics such as full name, age and date of birth, position in family, where they were brought up, by whom, and what, if any, schooling they had. Describe their physical appearance, with as many details as you can.

Next you could look at their disposition, whether calm or excitable, kind or brusque, thoughtful and cautious or impetuous and foolhardy. They will have both virtues and faults. They may be ambitious, or have secrets. There may be a previous romantic history, which need not be part of the plot but would help to mould the characters in your novel. What motivates them?

Consider what clothes and other objects such as food, music, books and animals are liked or disliked. What hobbies and interests do they have? Where do they live now, and with whom?

Then ask deeper questions, give the characters a twist, and find less obvious attributes. Keep away from stereotypes, apart from walk-ons who don't want to be noticeable by having any peculiarity.

Make your characters complex, with many different facets while still being recognisable. You could exaggerate something, or give them an obsession or something they are passionate about, to make them more interesting. If a character is going to behave in an especially odd manner, give clues early on, don't spring it on the unsuspecting reader without any warning.

Add any other features that might be useful and keep this outline ready to refer to when you are creating new characters.

If you have a large cast, or complicated family relationships, it might help to draw up family trees with dates of birth, marriage and death. You can see these in many books and they are often helpful to the reader, as well as the writer, in keeping track.

Draw diagrams of their houses and neighbourhoods, decorate and people them. This all helps to get to know your characters and their backgrounds.

However, do avoid the trap of putting all this into your novel. Like most other research it's for guidance, helps you to be accurate, propping up what's visible but not intruding. Only mention a fact when it's relevant.

Show your characters

You need to transfer your character profiles into your novel without being obvious. You cannot simply list the character's qualities in a descriptive passage. This would be boring, difficult for the reader to absorb, and unsubtle. In the same way as you come to know real people step by step, from what they are and do, you can portray your characters indirectly and gradually. A few telling details can make the reader aware of the main qualities instantly.

In *The Cobweb Cage* we discover something about Mrs Nugent through the way John sees her, the physical aspect, but also through what he knows of her, and this gives us several pertinent pieces of information.

John turned haggard eyes towards Mrs Nugent. She was a tall, slender woman with a sharp-featured face, but as he had reason to know her frowning appearance hid a kind and compassionate heart. Her servants were the best treated in the whole of Staffordshire and she worked tirelessly to raise money for miners' charities.

Later on a brief paragraph, again from *The Cobweb Cage*, gives us both an impression of what Johnny looks like and the skill Ivy has as an artist.

The drawing of Johnny was a bit lopsided, and his head was too big, but in some strange way Ivy had reproduced the features and the untidy hair so typical of her brother accurately enough for someone who knew him well to see the resemblance.

Indicating, by showing rather than telling, can be achieved by bringing in what they do now or have done in the past. It can be how they do things and why they do things. It can be through their beliefs, habits, hobbies, interests, tastes, preferences, what they say and how they say it.

You can show them through the eyes of other people, how other people see them, or talk about them and behave towards them.

Believe in your characters

They must be absolutely real to you or you won't make readers believe in them. Live with them, get inside them, know them as well as you possibly can. We all give something of ourselves when we write fiction, and though we might never commit murder we have to be able to know what it feels like to want to do it. We are complex people with good and bad points and our characters must be too.

Names are critical

They do far more than identify characters. Some authors cannot begin until they have named their cast. Names can tell you a great deal so make names appropriate.

Family names can indicate social background (Potter or Fitzharry) or ethnicity (O'Dowd or Singh). First names often indicate a character's age if it is associated with film stars (Marilyn or Clint) or an event or passing fashion (Mafeking or the Puritan names such as Charity).

Characters may be named after a relative or historical personage, which can say something about their parents, as do names which are either very popular or unusual.

Make sure your characters are easily differentiated by having some names short, some long, and of different rhythms or patterns, such as the stress on first or last syllable. Don't have the same initial letter for similar characters unless it's important to the plot, because it confuses readers.

If your story takes place in a real town, now or in the past, with a solicitor called Arnold Petheridge, make sure there isn't such a real person. Check telephone, commercial, street and professional directories.

Characters may be called something different by other characters. Mr Jones can be David, darling, daddy, grandpa, sir, or you bastard. The narrator should always refer to him by the same name, introduce him by that one, and make it obvious who is calling him by what variation.

Make names appropriate

An important feature of every novel is the choice of names. You cannot simply choose by sticking a pin in a general list. Names must fit the characters. In historicals the choice can be yet more crucial, as they must fit the times too.

Perceptions

There are many things which influence how we regard people, and the names they bear is only one, but an important one.

People

Those we have met in the past colour our attitudes, often subconsciously, towards others bearing the same name. Can you recall someone you disliked or feared at school or work? Do you select that name for your own children, or your fictional heroes or heroines? What about the names of people you like or admire? How do you regard the names of people you've read about, either fact or fiction? Is it to some extent related to what they are or do?

Sounds

Certain sounds, c, ch, sh, th, are gentle, soft, and names containing them appear gentle and soft too. Hard consonants such as k and p have different connotations. Hard vowel sounds indicate curtness, soft ones gentleness. Compare Jake and Janice.

Associations

Some names have obvious meanings, like Hardy, Strong, De'Ath, which may influence our perceptions. They are most often surnames, but some first names such as Patience or Randy can imply attributes, and one can think of fictional examples which have become synonyms for certain qualities, such as Scrooge in *A Christmas Carol*.

Writers need to be aware of different meanings in different countries. Randy, for example, is quite a common name in America, but in England has an unfortunate connotation. A girl emigrating to Australia was advised to change her name from Sheila because of the Aussie meaning.

Choosing first names

Names came to England from many other countries, at particular times, and you need to be aware of when a name came into common usage in the country you are writing about. These examples apply to the UK, but a similar set can be drawn up for other countries.

Fashions in names change. There are revivals of popularity and inventions of new names. Babies are named after contemporary heroes (Horatio) or heroines (Florence).

Ancient times

In earliest times names were simple descriptions but the meanings became more important, either for the qualities indicated or the associations with past or current people such as ancestors or pagan gods and goddesses.

The Greeks and Romans

Many Greek names, such as Iris or Basil, have connections with nature or with their myths. Roman names tended to have masculine and feminine forms, Julius and Julia.

The middle ages

The Normans introduced names from the north and the east and discouraged the use of many old Anglo-Saxon names. Biblical names and the names of saints became popular.

Modern times

Classical names revived in the Renaissance and the names of Catholic saints were less popular with Protestants after the Reformation, while Old Testament ones grew in favour. The Puritans often used the names of virtues such as Faith and Mercy, and had a short-lived fashion for descriptive names such as Praisegod Barebones. The heroine of Diana Norman's *The Vizard Mask* starts life as Penitence.

There was more variety in the eighteenth century. There was a revival of Anglo-Saxon names, perhaps because of the Hanoverian influence, and the use of Latin forms such as Emilia or Maria. In late Victorian times flower and jewel names were popular. Many surnames were used as first names – Bruce, Duncan, Douglas.

The entertainment industry, with the invented or abbreviated names of film and stage stars, has produced brief popularity, such as for Bebe or Clint, but many more names have appeared in the last hundred years, often from other countries.

Be timely

For both the first and surnames you plan to use, check they were around and reasonably popular for the time. In some eras inventions of new names would have been acceptable, but not in others. There are several dictionaries of names on the market which give meanings and derivations, and the history of usage. It is wise to have on your bookshelves at least one for first names, and one for surnames.

Selecting surnames

These developed in the middle ages, and there are four broad categories. There are many thousands of names within them and a great deal of change and corruption of spellings which sometimes makes it difficult to be sure of the original meanings.

Many names in the past occurred in fairly limited areas, so it is wise to check names you intend to use against their geographical distribution. If they are names from other countries, check when they first came to England, such as Le Fanu with Huguenot refugees of the seventeenth century, Jewish names in the 1930s, or Polish during World War II.

Ancestral

These are based on the name of a parent, for example Jackson.

Territorial

Places of origin, mainly villages or towns, but also less specific names such as Greenhill come under this heading. In many of Georgette Heyer's novels you will find several characters named after places. Sometimes you can even spot the area on the map, which she may have used for inspiration.

Occupational

Smith is the obvious one, but there are many others often deriving from now-obsolete trades.

Descriptive

These can be nicknames reflecting the original owner's appearance, such as Short, or habits, Dolittle, or even morals, Sleigh (Sly).

Be appropriate

You can suggest the social standing of your characters by choice of names. This is often a matter or perception rather than historical accuracy. Servants would often be called by diminutives such as Ben or Meg. At some times they would be addressed only by their surnames by their employers.

The upper classes would be more likely to have fancier first names, though in the twentieth century this does not apply to the invented names of film or pop stars. You can imply an aristocratic connection by choosing one of the family names of peers, like Howard or Talbot. Occupational names imply a lower class.

Specifying buildings

Inns and houses and some other buildings can be given particular names. It adds reality to your novel to use these but, unless you want to use a real building, take care not to copy existing names like Chatsworth or Blenheim, and ensure you don't have a Royal Oak prior to Charles II's sojourn in an oak tree.

You may want to identify a castle or a manor house by adding the place name, but often you can just say The Manor or The Rectory or a posting house without being more specific.

Do some research on the development of house and inn names. Try to find out when street numbering began or when houses were given identifying names other than such as 'Ma Parry's Cottage'.

Naming animals

In the days of horse transport you may specify names for horses. Other animals such as dogs may have names too. Take as much care choosing for them as for people, since the choices will be those of your characters and arise from their likes and perceptions.

Keep track

Start to keep a card index of the names you use, so that as you go on to write several books, especially if they are set in the same time, you avoid repeating names. You can use differently coloured index cards for male and female first names, surnames, buildings and animals. If you come across especially appropriate names for use in another book, you could list them separately for consultation later. Make lists of names which you might use, now or in the future.

Know the relationships

These are the various connections between your characters and you need to know how they work, what drives them or causes conflict. What do they feel about one another? Have they any past history which could influence what they do now? Do they have conflicting motives?

You will know all this so that you get the atmosphere between characters right, but don't fall into the trap of telling the reader all about it. Let it emerge gradually, during the course of conversations, by what they say themselves or by comments from other characters who may know.

Keep protagonists on-stage

The protagonists, the most important characters, should be on-stage as much as possible. Keep them busy. They should be given most to do, be active and make things happen, not simply react to events. They must solve the mystery, tackle the villain and perform the heroic tasks. They should not be there performing a minor role while a subsidiary character takes the limelight or does something heroic, which your main character could have done.

Their aims must be laudable, they must face and overcome difficulties and they must be strong though vulnerable. As well as admirable characteristics they must have some faults too. Some imperfections can be attractive, and even murder by a hero could be acceptable in a good cause, such as destroying a terrorist.

The faults of your sympathetic characters should be those the reader will feel are minor and human, the kind of thing they are prepared to admit to themselves. They might accept impatience, unpunctuality or untidiness, but they would not approve of unkindness or petty thieving. Perfectly good characters tend to be flat, as do perfectly evil ones. Rounded ones have faults as well as virtues.

Provide conflict

Whatever the cause of conflict, readers must care about the result. What's at stake has to be important, to matter greatly, and there must be opposition. The protagonists or opposing sides have different aims, which cannot both be achieved although the reader may want this. Then a satisfactory solution or compromise has to be found.

There can also be inner conflict when one character has contradictory objectives. Know the conflicts, both internal and external, which the characters face.

This is often indicated in the first paragraphs of a novel. In *The Baron's Bride*, there is more than a hint of future conflict between Eva and her father.

> *Eva sat calmly on the stool, her head bowed, but beneath her outward submissiveness she boiled with anger and resentment. After a few moments she raised her eyes, now icily blue, and glanced through long, thick lashes at her father who stood near the narrow window looking down into the outer bailey.*

On the other hand we can have inner conflict, or fighting against circumstances, such as in *Royal Courtship*, where Isabella is in danger from the most powerful man in the Kingdom.

> *'Would that I could dance with you, Mistress Davenport! But I fear - this leg of mine is troublesome. I shall give myself the pleasure of watching, however, the loveliest young lady at Court. Now let me see - boy!'*
>
> *Isabella Davenport gave way to treasonable thoughts. What horrid misfortune was it that had brought her to the notice of this gross mountain of a man now sitting on the throne of England?*

Establish the relative importance of the conflicts in the novel. One of lesser importance may be the origin of a sub-plot.

Create sympathy for your protagonists

A character is 'sympathetic' when the reader believes in him, likes him, can imagine being him, approves his aims or wants him to achieve them. Readers approve of protagonists who are admirable, dependable and generous. They loathe bullying or ruthless greed, though they may be fascinated by such characters and enjoy the frisson of meeting them.

Heroes and heroines in particular need to be sympathetic and have strengths which are attractive. If your protagonist has only unpleasant or despicable traits most readers won't identify with him, although they might understand him. If a protagonist is a victim he must still be strong, it shouldn't be his own fault and he mustn't give up. His sacrifices must be worthwhile.

Let your characters take over

Cardboard characters, two-dimensional characters, are puppets which the author pushes around. If you have created truly believable people you may find that your plans for them aren't compatible with how they are. Then you need to adjust either the character or the plot. One story may work with a certain character but not with others.

Authors who create characters and follow where they lead know this, and their books don't depend a great deal on plot. Authors who rely too much on a preordained plot may find their characters wooden and incredible. Most novels are a balance.

Make your characters grow

Many changes occur as time passes, such as marriage and children, different houses and jobs, but we also change in response to experiences. Your characters must too. They must be different at the end of the story because of the conflict and its resolution, and this difference can be an improvement or not but it must be believable. Often the apparent change is a discovery, a stripping away of a surface disguise to the real character beneath.

Questions to answer and things to do

1. Make a list of all your characters in order of importance, with a brief description of each. They will be the protagonists, main characters, minor characters and walk-ons.
2. For the protagonists and major characters, draw up profiles. Keep these handy for reference and to add to them.
3. If it's appropriate, draw up family trees of the relationships of your characters or some of them.
4. Try to find pictures of real people who look like your characters and put them on a board where you can look at them. They can be cut from newspapers, magazines, maps or photocopied from biographies. There are Internet sites which allow you to change hairstyles, so modern characters can be made to look like people in older centuries.
5. As you write, make notes of any new facets of characters that occur to you. Add these to profiles. They will help you keep on track so that actions and feelings are consistent with your characters.
6. Make lists of names common at the time you're writing about.

Construct a table from your own acquaintances or from fictional sources of names which have particular associations for you. Do this for both first and surnames, and alongside each name put what the association is and whatever reasons you can think of for making that association.

Name	Association	Reasons

Choose two or three appropriate (but not too obvious) first names for both men and women born in each of the past ten centuries.

In which century would the following names be most likely to be popular in England, and why?

1. Bertram
2. Caroline
3. Darren
4. Faithful
5. George
6. Henrietta
7. Karen
8. Pearl
9. Tancred
10. Victoria

Complete this chart, and using each letter of the alphabet, try and find surnames from each of the four categories. You then have a long enough list to make sure that you vary the names used for your characters. You may be excused difficult letters such as Q, and XYZ, though there are a few for all except X!

	Ancestral	Territorial	Occupational	Descriptive
A	Adamson	Aldridge	Archer	Armstrong
B				

Many names have variations that may be used in different classes of society. Suggest variations of the following which would more likely be used in the lower classes:

Name	Variations or diminutives
1. Albert	
2. Clarice	
3. Edward	
4. Eleanor	
5. Elizabeth	
6. John	
7. Margaret	
8. Millicent	
9. Richard	
10. William	

Find more with similar variations

Go back through all the names you have chosen and decide, for both first and surnames, which of the following characters it is most appropriate for, giving reasons:

hero or heroine/ friends/ villains/ major characters/ minor characters/ walk-on parts.

Name   Type of character   Reasons:

Tips by example

Brief start to a profile of Marion:

Marion Jenkins, born 2nd September 1935, aged 16 in June 1951 when the book starts.

Lived in Birmingham all her life, with parents William and Jane and older brother Thomas. At first in a small terraced house in an inner city area then moved in 1946 to a large detached house in a leafy outer suburb.

Educated at a small local primary school, then to a girls' grammar school where her favourite subjects were science, tennis and art.

Of medium height, athletic but with a tendency to put on weight, straight blonde hair worn short with a fringe, pale blue eyes, a snub nose and full lips. Her chin is determined.

Key points

1. Characters vary in importance.
2. You need to know more about them than you will use.
3. Make sure there is conflict.
4. Create sympathetic protagonists.

5

Characters 2 – circumstances change

Circumstances can be different in different times and places

People are the same everywhere and at all times. They have the same feelings but may differ in how they can behave.

For example, the position of women has varied enormously over the centuries. Social hierarchies have been different, sometimes centred on the King's Court, sometimes elsewhere. The powers of tribal leaders, barons, squires and landlords have varied. In older times the influence of priests was very important. In new countries like America and Australia there will have been different hierarchies and attitudes to those in Europe.

In this chapter we will discuss how to make characters believable by using their roles within the constraints of the plot, attitudes, religious, moral and other beliefs. We will also look at speech, mannerisms and costume.

Have characters which fit their times

However the original idea for your plot and choice of the time setting occurs, you need to research many aspects and see how they fit into your plot – or adjust your plot in the light of such research. Your characters must fit into that time. They must be enclosed by their time, not just in a physical respect, such as modes of travel, but also in non-physical restrictions.

You would not have physical anachronisms such as aeroplanes and telephones in Tudor times. Anachronistic attitudes are equally serious mistakes but more difficult to control.

Conventional behaviour

Your characters have to abide by the conventions of their time. To write a believable historical story you have to understand and make use of the contemporary attitudes and beliefs, not superimpose those of a later century.

This can pose a dilemma because modern readers like their characters, especially heroines, to be strong and independent. In many past ages women simply did not have the chance, or the options, that a modern woman has. Writers have to steer a course between reality and expectations. It is possible to have strong women – there are many real examples of such – but the limitations they face are things to be aware of all the time.

If characters go against accepted norms, you must be very sure of their motives, and know what would be the reaction of other people. What would be the arguments used, and the consequences? Such behaviour can be a fruitful source of conflict.

Be aware of attitudes

Some attitudes seem the same in all centuries, such as the contempt of old men for the youth of today. *'Things were not like that when I was a lad.'* Others, however, vary at different times, so you have to be aware of what is normal for the time you have chosen.

In *The Cobweb Cage*, we see the perceptions about what is or is not suitable work for a man, and in what circumstances.

> *'I wonder if I could make bread?' he asked suddenly, and Marigold looked at him in surprise.*
>
> *'Bread?' she exclaimed. 'But baking's a woman's job.'*
>
> *'Not where the bread's made for selling. I suddenly thought of that chap Foster, at Heath Hayes. He and his family run a shop, and he bakes the bread as well as working at the pit.'*

Class

Ask the following questions.

Do people regard their station in life as unalterable? Is it ordained by God? If it is, would they ever consider trying to change it, or would such attempts be frowned upon? This could cause conflict if one member of the family is dissatisfied and tries to 'rise above his station', perhaps becoming too proud to acknowledge his poorer relations if he is successful.

Is there any possible class-mobility? Can the shopkeeper or factory owner, however rich, be accepted as a gentleman and mix with the upper classes or the aristocracy?

If mobility is possible, how can it be achieved? Where it is possible to be upwardly mobile, is this through education, wealth or marriage? And don't forget, there could be downward mobility too.

In *Heir to Rowanlea*, Harry has just proposed.

> 'You know that it is useless, Harry, and I have told you above a dozen times that Papa would never permit me to marry you, not as matters stand,' Elizabeth replied, patting her immaculate curls and smiling provocatively at him.
>
> 'What has he against me? I'll admit I have no title, and my expectations are no match for your fortune, but there might be Rowanlea! It seems more than probably.'
>
> 'Might!' Elizabeth repeated. 'That is the rub. Although I have no need to marry a rich man, Papa says that it is wrong to marry anyone who cannot equal it, and he, or rather it is Mama, has set her heart on my acquiring a title.'

How do members of different classes treat one another? Can they mix freely? Are there conventions to be observed, by all sides?

A frequent remark, usually aggrieved, is that a person's class could not be discerned from the clothes they wore.

Status

What is the hierarchy of, for example, different occupations or professions? Does this change at different times? Surgeons, for instance, began as barbers or sawbones, a lower-class occupation. Nursing before Florence Nightingale was not a suitable occupation for girls from the middle classes. Such middle-class girls had very few options if they had to earn a living.

What is the hierarchy of servants or retainers? Who is more important in a large house – butler, steward or housekeeper?

If the relative positions and powers are not clearly defined they can be a source of conflict.

Is status connected with wealth, or other considerations such as education, sex, or occupation? It differs at different times.

Women

What is the position of married and unmarried women in society? In many times and places unmarried girls have been very restricted in what they were permitted to do, but this often depended on class. While the upper and middle classes were never allowed out unchaperoned, working-class girls had of necessity more freedom. Wives had certain duties, but were also constrained by rules of what they could not do.

In *Heir to Rowanlea*, an older woman is talking about men.

'They like to believe themselves the masters, and to be able to consider us weak creatures who would be utterly lost without their guidance,' Lady Weare went on musingly. 'They are totally inconsistent, of course, for when it comes to running a household we are expected to be able to make judgements and take decisions without the slightest reference to them. Indeed, most men would be highly offended to be consulted on such matters as employing another laundry maid, or ordering a dinner for their guests! Yet when it concerns other questions, of religion, or politics, or even choice of wines, we are held to be incapable of ever learning anything about the matter! Fortunately men are so satisfied with the state of affairs that they never think to consider how we are really managing them!'

What control do women have over property? Could they do as they wished with it or did it automatically belong to their husbands? If they were widowed, did male trustees have control? What control do they have over their children? Could they, for instance, determine how and by whom they were educated, or who they married, or was this the province of fathers or other male relatives?

How may this vary for women in different classes? In *Campaign for a Bride*, the twelve-year-old Barbara is to have an arranged marriage.

> *'Am I to go and live in Hereford?' Barbara asked a trifle apprehensively.*
>
> *'No. Normally you would have gone to live with my mother while I go to France, but she is so ill that your father and I have agreed 'tis best to leave you here until you are old enough for me to claim you.'*

The Scarlet Letter is based on the custom, in Puritan New England, of forcing a woman accused of adultery to wear a scarlet 'A' on her bodice. Men were not similarly shamed. Sexual behaviour for woman has usually been controlled far more strictly than for men.

Other

How do people of your time regard the following issues, for example? You can probably think of more where attitudes change at different times.

Are they afraid of foreigners, or contemptuous, believing them inferior, or amused by their differences?

Slavery has often, in many places, been regarded as normal and perhaps the only way of cultivating the plantations or doing certain jobs. At other times it has been condemned as reprehensible.

Throughout history there have been many empires, but was the acquisition or building of an Empire regarded as for the glory of the conquerors or the monarch, for power, for control over resources or for military security? Missionaries regarded empires as opening up opportunities for converting or educating the natives of conquered lands. These reasons vary in, for example, Roman, Tudor and Victorian times.

Was warfare glorified or deplored? Was patriotism, pride in one's country, something to be proud of or deplored as jingoism?

Who needed education? Many wealthy men of earlier times did not want to know how to read or write because they had scribes or clerks who could do it for them. Frequently, women were not expected to be educated, and sometimes those who were gained unenviable reputations and may have lessened their chances of marriage.

Was scientific or technical progress condemned or approved? Did people see the benefits or were they concerned only with the disadvantages? Were they afraid of new things? Steam, railways, the use of gas and electricity, new medical procedures such as anaesthetics or vaccination had their opponents as well as supporters.

All of these things could produce fierce conflict.

Be conscious of beliefs

Certain things which may be widely questioned today would have been commonly accepted beliefs in the past. Only the very occasional rebel would have disagreed openly with these beliefs, and many people who might have doubted them would have done so secretly.

These beliefs would have a big influence on behaviour, on what was allowed, or practicable, right and acceptable, or wrong and to be condemned.

Religion

Christianity, religious observance, the literal truth of the Bible, the Ten Commandments, were common beliefs in Europe for many centuries. There were monasteries and convents, monks and nuns, saints and miracles and, for many, religion was inextricably entwined with everything.

The Christian year had prescribed seasons and festivals, with associated observances. See how these are used in the *Brother Cadfael Chronicles*. People believed in an afterlife and hellfire, which could influence their actions in this life. They also believed in spirits.

Religious differences, whether between Christian, Jew or Muslim, or Catholic and Protestant, could be fierce, and in many times and places there was no mutual tolerance.

Moral

In Europe, correct behaviour and the legal system were based on the Ten Commandments, and in the past moral attitudes were often much clearer and more universally accepted than they are today. Punishments for wrongdoers were severe.

With a deterrent of hanging for minor infringements of the law or social ostracism for disregarding a moral code, what forces impelled people to take the risk? Was it ignorance, carelessness, arrogance or desperation? You need to know what imperatives drive your characters in situations very unlike those of today.

Social

Behaviour towards others was often dictated by one's social position and how much economic or other power was involved. Compare the different ways a feudal baron and his villeins or serfs would treat one another, or landlord and tenant, mill owner and weaver, squire and villager, aristocrat and merchant, old families and the nouveau riche.

Men of the cloth were respected, but according to their own hierarchy. Bishops outranked vicars, curates and Nonconformists were much lower down. Men of religions other than Christianity would pose problems of acceptance or precedence in a Christian society.

Social differences were accepted as natural or ordained, and deference was expected and given. Look at books of etiquette for the correct manner of addressing different people and orders of precedence on formal occasions.

Political

Before universal suffrage, direct action to express their feelings was often the only way open to non-voters. There were the various rebellions like the Peasants' Revolt, rioters such as the Luddites, and movements such as Chartism and the Trade Unions. They adopted different tactics.

Many of these protests were concerned with social, living or industrial conditions more than democracy. You need to know about them and how different people regarded them, as well as knowing the actions of kings or ministers or parliaments.

You also need to know of events and movements in other countries which might influence your plot, and be aware that the same stages of development – technical, political and others were not always reached at the same time in different countries.

Know what's possible

Based on the current attitudes and beliefs of the time you have selected as the background to your plot, you must make characters true to their time in their own beliefs and behaviour.

Pregnancy

A familiar dilemma throughout the ages has been an unmarried girl becoming pregnant. There were different options open to her at various times, and what she did might depend on her social position or the wealth of her family. It could also depend on the attitude and resources of the child's father.

Wealthy men who had seduced poor girls might pay for her to be cared for. They might recognise the child, even take it into their own household or give the mother an allowance. Or they might marry her off, inducing some other man to take responsibility and accept the child by providing a dowry.

Girls of all classes without the help of the father might seek abortions, but in the past these would be illegal, often involve dangerous drugs and often prove fatal.

Generally the poorer families cared less about illegitimacy but would, when practicable, force the couple to marry before the child was born. If this did not happen either the children would be left in orphanages or simply absorbed into a large family. Sometimes a young grandmother would pretend to be the mother if they cared about respectability or wanted the girl to have a chance of marriage.

In other classes, if marriage was not possible, there were various solutions aimed at hiding the family's 'shame'. A drastic option was to turn the sinful girl adrift, often to starve or turn to prostitution. Note that it was often the family's decision, not the girl's, because she was usually dependent on them for financial support.

In pre-Reformation times upper class girls might be spirited away to a convent, sometimes to spend the rest of their lives there, sometimes to return without the child, who might have been fostered.

In the eighteenth, nineteenth and early twentieth century, they might be sent away during the pregnancy and the child given for adoption or placed in an orphanage.

As late as 1940, most babies born out of wedlock were placed for adoption, and it was comparatively rare for an unmarried girl to admit to the fact of her child and keep it. This was largely because without financial support it was impracticable.

In the late twentieth century there was legal abortion and no stigma attached to children born to single mothers, so that many women (and couples) opted to have children without marriage.

Speech and narration

We specifically discuss dialogue techniques in a later chapter, but it is important both in speech and narrative to give the right flavour of the time without being incomprehensible.

Try to avoid glaring inaccuracies and anachronisms, such as a character being mesmerised before Dr. Mesmer, or saying something was not his cup of tea before this drink came to England.

Above all make the meaning clear. Writing in Saxon or medieval English would be impossible for most of us, and we'd find no readers. There are ways of keeping the narrative timely while expressed clearly in suitable language. Make it formal and straightforward without being either archaic or too obviously present day. Use imagery that would be within the common experience of your characters. Avoid modern phrases, jargon or slang terms.

Mannerisms and manners

Characters can demonstrate moods or characteristics by mannerisms such as drumming their fingers on a table, chewing the end of a pencil, compulsive eating of sweets or cigarette smoking. Find things, for example objects or clothes which relate to the specific time, and use these to display mannerisms. When men wore long-haired wigs they could play with curls. When they wore swords they could hold the hilts, or with daggers toss them in the air. When people wrote with quills the feathers could be used to stroke faces. Snuff-takers could adopt various techniques. Fans had a whole language of their own.

Manners were important too. Ladies would expect deference from men. Humble folk would stand aside and doff their hats or curtsey to the squire. Children might be seen but not heard. Table manners differed through the centuries, from eating with a knife, belching in appreciation, or men wearing their hats in the house. Times of meals varied, as did the seating arrangements at table and the way food was presented.

Dress your characters properly

There are many books on historical costume and it is simple to research the details. This is not all you need to do. Think yourself into the current fashions. Costume can do more than provide decoration. Be aware of how particular styles can affect behaviour or movement.

In *Her Captive Cavalier*, during a sword fight dress was important to the outcome.

> *(Robert) wore just his shirt, tucked firmly into tight-fitting breeches, and was in stocking feet.*
>
> *This, she soon realised, gave him an advantage over John Culham, encumbered with a heavy riding coat and boots. He could move with greater speed over the stone-flagged floor, while Culham more than once found his feet slipping on the smooth stone and had to pause to regain his balance.*

In *Cavalier Courtship*, Caroline has borrowed boys' clothing.

Robby cupped his hands for her foot, and she sprang into the saddle. She had never before been so unrestricted with clothing, and it gave her a new confidence, so that as she walked Silver through the gateway and on to the drive which led to the road, she had a jaunty air which became her slim figure and boyish looks.

It isn't just clothing. Outside circumstances can influence what your characters are able to do. In *The Glowing Hours*, they want to go to Paris.

'But we can't go while there's a general strike and almost no trains and boats.'

Work these special differences into your background detail or plot, and make sure your characters can physically do what you ask of them. For example, ladies wearing tightly laced corsets and long, trailing skirts are much less mobile than modern women in jeans and trainers. Panniers, bustles and crinolines all constricted movement, as did tight or hobbled skirts, but in different ways.

Medieval headdresses or wide hats have to be considered. Clerics and monks in long skirts move differently from men in trousers. Shawls and plaids can be used for many unusual purposes.

Remember

There may be a conflict between something a man of the sixteenth century would do, accept or believe in, and the sympathy or empathy your twentieth-century reader will feel for his beliefs and consequent actions. You need to find ways in which you can deal with this, to make your reader understand without direct exposition.

Questions to answer and things to do

1. Put markers in reference books you may use frequently, so that you can find pages quickly, for costume or dates or maps and so on. Post-It note markers in different colours can be very useful.

2. When your novel is finished, ask whether your main characters have changed in some way. They need to, or there is no point in writing about them. It may be just age and wisdom, or acceptance of the inevitable, or limitations or failure. It may be growth of arrogance if more powerful or greater determination to succeed. But make it sympathetic! Readers must understand why the changes happen and accept the reasons, even if they can't approve the changes.

3. Make a point of observing people, how they talk and behave. Especially small gestures, which you can use to make characters recognisable and memorable.

Tips by example

The following are a few extracts from the first month of Pepys' diary (January 1660) to illustrate some of the points made above.

> *...sat with Mr Ashwell talking and singing till 9 a-clock....We then fell to cards till dark...sat with me till 10 at night at cards.....Parliament spent this day in fast and prayer.....much troubled with my nose, which was much swelled....the venison pasty was palpable beef, which was not handsome...to Mrs Jem and found her in bed, and some was afraid that it would prove the small-pox...overtaking Captain Oakshott in his silk cloak, whose sword got hold of many people in walking...thence home, where I found my wife and maid a-washing...I then went to bed and left my wife and the maid a-washing still...at Kinsington, we understood how my Lord Chesterfield had killed another gentleman about half an hour before and was fled.*

Key points

1. Characters must fit in with their times.
2. Attitudes and beliefs vary in different times and places.
3. Speech, manners and dress must be appropriate.
4. Characters must change by the end of the novel.

6 Plot – the all-important middle

Five stages of a plot

First the problem needs to be stated, and this is done as early as possible in the novel.

The second and longest stage is the development, the bulk of the book, which must be compelling enough to make readers want to know what happens.

Then comes the major crisis or turning point, often when a decision has to be made or a battle won, and this is best as close to the end as possible.

The denoncement follows, with any necessary explanations which cannot be made earlier, and sub-plots wrapped up, again only those which cannot be ended earlier. Suppose there is a literal battle, part of an explanation might be factors that the winners, and probably the readers, do not know beforehand, but which help their cause. A sub-plot might be that an enemy of a major character is killed and no longer a threat to him.

Finally comes the resolution, which must be strong and satisfying. The man gets the girl, the sleuth unmasks the murderer or the soldier captures the castle. It helps if you know the resolution so that you have something to work towards, but you may not know the precise path by which you reach it until you write the middle of the novel.

Good middles make novels great

We've looked at some opening paragraphs and how to begin a novel successfully. If you get the opening right, introduce the main characters, set up the situation, establish the theme and a good conflict, and have some idea of where you are going and know, if only roughly, the end or resolution of your novel, the rest should be easy. Shouldn't it?

Not necessarily. It's comparatively easy to write good openings and satisfying endings, but it's the middle that makes novels good and distinguishes good writers from average ones. You have to make the reader stay with you, carry them through it, enticing them all the way, maintaining the momentum of the story and keeping up the interest and tension, with them eager to know the outcome.

The middle must be compulsive reading but this is often the most difficult part to write. It's fatally easy to lose one's way, having too little to say or padding with more and more incidents which don't help the story.

What readers want

When I ask readers and editors what makes a good novel, they say a convincing plot and good characters, but they have other suggestions. Most people say they want to be entertained. This means a good plot, absorbing, exciting, a fast pace, page-turning quality, one they can't put down, as well as convincing characters and good writing.

Perhaps the most telling requirement is for a book that they are prepared to recommend to others.

Other points are some knowledge conveyed, an interesting setting and a subject which interests the reader. These apply especially to historicals.

The shape of a plot

Whether you plan the whole story in detail or let your characters and plot develop, you need to be aware of the overall shape. It is something to consider as you go along. You can put it right when you are revising, though it may involve a lot of rewriting at that stage.

Crises

The shape of the novel consists of a series of crises, each gradually or suddenly developed, then at some point, not necessarily immediately, resolved. Some will be small, some huge. The resolution of one crisis will often lead to a further complication and eventually another crisis, and all will lead to the major crisis or turning point, as close to the end of the novel as possible.

In *The Cobweb Cage*, for example, when the father is injured the mother has to go out to work, so Marigold looks after the younger children and Ivy is injured. Marigold blames herself, so later on is indulgent with her sister while Ivy resents Marigold and cheats her.

Think of the old rhyme, *'For want of a nail the shoe was lost,'* and then the horse, battle, and finally the kingdom.

Decide which are going to be the big scenes, the main crises or turning points of the plot, and plan how you will work up to them. Don't have them too close together – intersperse with minor scenes and lesser crises.

Peaks and troughs

You can imagine the plot as a line on a graph, with the level of intensity on the vertical axis, and the progress of the novel, either in time or chapter divisions, along the horizontal axis, and the plot line moving in a series of peaks and troughs. Each peak is a crisis. Have one near the start, then there will be a few big ones, lots of smaller ones in between, and finally the biggest of all as close to the end as possible.

The Shape of a Plot and Sub-plot

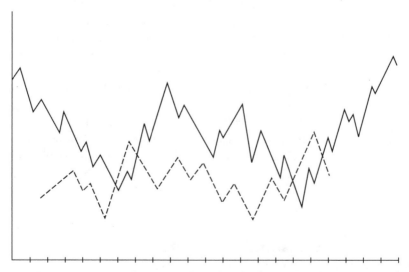

The vertical axis indicates the level of intensity, and the horizontal one shows chapter divisions. The unbroken line is the main plot, with ups and downs, but major important scenes near the start, the end, and the middle of the novel. The broken line is a sub-plot, with similar ups and downs, but not so important, and the whole lasting for a shorter time, ending before the final crisis of the main plot.

Pre-planning

It is advisable, but not absolutely essential, for beginners to draw up at least an outline of what is likely to happen, to save going too far off track. It could cause months of rewriting if you don't decide beforehand whether your plot can work, whether the timescale fits in, whether you can get your characters in the right places when you need them there. It also helps to see whether you have a sufficiently strong plot in the first place, since without this you won't have a publishable novel.

If you have only a sketchy plan, don't worry. Writers differ enormously in how they work, including how much they plan ahead. Many have little or no idea of what will come next. Many say that when they start they know where they are going, but not the route by which they get there. Others write vast outlines.

To help you refine your ideas and know what the novel is about, try to express the basic plot in one sentence.

Sub-plots too

You may have sub-plots to deal with. They need to be woven in, like a plait. Some of them could be brief, soon resolved, or lasting almost as long as the main plot. They can involve the main characters directly, or only slightly, or concern only the minor characters, or a combination of both. They need developments, ups and downs, crises and resolutions in the same way as the main plot.

Sub-plots will have similar peaks and troughs, as in the diagram, but remember to spread them out. You should not have all the characters involved in major crises at the same time, and the sub-plots have to be finished before the main one or you risk having the ending of the book weak, an anticlimax.

Plots and sub-plots

The main strand or storyline is that concerning your chief characters, but you will, especially in a long historical, be likely to have several sub-plots. You need to weave them together so that the different stories or sub-plots converge and separate, meet and overlap throughout the novel. They will affect one another and may mirror or contrast one another.

In *The Glowing Hours*, I have three girls who become friends. Nell is from a very poor background, contrasting with Kitty whose family are wealthy. Nell is escaping from a vicious father, while the third girl, Gwyneth, is running away from an overbearing one.

Don't be in too much of a rush to introduce sub-plots. Let your readers become familiar with your main characters and involved with them before you leave the main plot-line to follow other separate sub-plots. And before you do this, get the readers interested in the characters who will be involved in the sub-plot.

Space them out

Some sub-plots may be ended quite early, but make sure you don't introduce a sub-plot, concentrate exclusively on it, and solve it in a few pages. That destroys tension and anticipation, and readers don't like being kept away from the protagonists for too long. Instead prolong the sub-plots by inserting bits of them into the main narrative at intervals.

On the other hand, don't introduce a sub-plot and forget to continue with it for so long that your readers have forgotten the details by the time you come back to it. If the story demands that it is drawn-out, be sure to mention it occasionally to keep it in the reader's mind.

Keep track

It helps to keep a list of your scenes, just a few brief words to remind you of what they did and who is taking part. Then you can see quickly if you've left one character or sub-plot out for too long, or concentrated too much on one sub-plot for a while at the expense of others.

In the example overleaf, I kept track of my characters by having the date of each scene in the first column, the characters in the scene (shown by initials to save space) in the second, and a very brief note of what happens in the third.

By glancing down the second column, when the story becomes more complex later on, I can soon see whether I have left one sub-plot out for too long, or had too many scenes close together featuring a less important character.

Summary of
Chapters –
Cobweb Cage
▼

DATE	Main Chars	
		Chapter one p 1
2/1901	M	Marigold alone – Poppy born – locked in pantry
2/01	MJyMyJ	Johnny finds her – discuss names
1/05	My	Ivy born – nightmares – flowers – names appropriate
12/08	J	pit accident
2/09	My	John home and ill – Mary goes to work
3/09	P	Poppy wants to go on choir outing
4/09	MI	Mrs Tasker brings Ivy home with pie – falls on fire
		Chapter two p 35
4/09	Fam	Ivy's accident – burnt
/10	MI	Ivy resists school – effects of burns on John – Johnny brings delicacies home
3/11	Fam	Ivy draws – job for Marigold – Johnny brings meat – wants drawing – Mary backache
5/11	Fam	Walk on hills – talk of unions and reforms
6/11	My	Mary home – pregnant – il – Mrs Nugent calls – Mary miscarries
6/11	Jy	Johnny a thief – sent to job in Birmingham

Have you enough plot for a compulsive, page-turning middle?

Editors are looking for that something extra, which will make your book stand out from the pile. Having intrigued readers with the first few paragraphs and pages, you need to keep their interest through the middle of the book.

If you have different characters, not stock ones which can be found in so many unpublished novels, editors will look favourably on your novel. These sort of characters help you writing it, too. They won't behave in predictable ways, so waiting to see what they will do keeps the reader interested. This could help you with the plotting.

Ask what the characters would do

Always ask, at each turning point of time or decision, what this particular character would do. For example, facing an enemy, the weak man might run away and thereby escape, or he might dither and have to fight, which he does badly and is therefore captured or injured, which will turn the story in a different direction to the one he perhaps planned.

A brave, hot-headed man might fight against overwhelming odds and be injured or killed, but if he were wiser he might hide in order to face the enemy at a time more favourable to himself. The characters and circumstances will determine what happens.

The protagonists

In many historicals there are both male and female protagonists, and as a form of shorthand we call them hero and heroine. In general heroes should be fascinating, attractive, exciting, they may be funny or witty, but are different. Tall, dark and handsome is a cliché. Give them something extra. If you are writing any kind of romantic fiction, where there is a strong love story and the main focus of attention is the heroine, it isn't always possible or necessary to introduce the hero immediately, but it helps to bring him in fairly soon. Heroines need to be strong, feisty and independent. By no means have them weepy or clinging.

If this is a male-dominated novel – a war or adventure setting with few if any women – your hero, as well as your heroine in love stories, must be likeable, someone with whom the reader feels instant sympathy and whose objectives are laudable. In war and adventure stories there may be only minor roles for women, with no obvious heroine playing a big part in the action. Then the usual situation is the good guy – the protagonist – struggling in some way against the bad guy – the antagonist.

Aims

Your protagonists need to have aims and objectives for which they strive. These aims will be limited by the extent of the knowledge they have and the physical restrictions of the times. A girl wanting independence cannot become a governess unless she has been taught various accomplishments herself. A crofter in Scotland cannot improve his land when he is dispossessed of it during the Highland Clearances.

If you incorporate real events into your story, the aims of the characters must fit in with what happened. You can give them a fictional role in bringing about some event or preventing something else, but when readers know what has actually happened you cannot use the event as a surprise outcome.

In my civil war novels I have used fictional heroes to take vital messages, and a girl as a spy. Both could have influenced the real outcome.

You need other aims which fit in, such as remaining alive in a battle, rescuing someone, escaping or killing an enemy.

Motives

Many motives of revenge, jealousy or personal gain will be present at all times, but to what extent and how might your characters allow their motives to determine their actions? How will circumstances influence them?

The all-important conflict

The strength of any novel depends on the importance of the conflict, either between the characters or within a character. The situation, promising lots of conflict and tension, needs to be established soon, but it cannot be something which is resolved quickly. Nor should it be so trivial that a sensible discussion or easy solution would resolve it in the first chapter. It must be important, complicated and have several aspects. Conflict is not just argument, rows and constant sniping at one another.

If you have a setting which is original or treated in an unusual manner, it adds interest and sometimes mystery to the novel.

Internal conflict

This happens when characters have conflicting desires, or cannot please two people with different expectations of them. Which do they choose? How do they decide? Doing one thing might cause great anguish to them or to people they love, who depend on them or who admire them. They need to weigh up the options and they won't always make the best choice. This can cause problems in the future.

The Cobweb Cage shows Marigold with the dilemma of being needed by her parents, but with no money to support them unless she gives up her son. She has to make the agonising decision.

External conflict

This is where the protagonist cannot control the circumstances because other people have their own actions, or the external world gets in the way.

In historicals it can often be a real event which hinders the characters or ruins their plans. Their side may lose the battle or they could be trapped in a siege. This can be an impassable road or a fearful storm. Sometimes the protagonist cannot overcome these obstacles so has to find another way of achieving his or her wishes.

It may not be a physical restraint. Psychological pressure might be brought to persuade the protagonists to do things they would not wish to do.

Conflicts

How might the causes of conflict differ at different periods? Religious and political and sexual differences will vary with time.

Whatever this conflict is, it must be important, something big at stake, and readers must care about it. Often there is a situation where there are opposing aims, both of which the reader wants to see achieved, but this is impossible so that a satisfactory compromise or solution must be found.

Some reasons for conflict

Some could come out of the characters themselves if, for instance, they are very different in background, values or attitudes, or have differing ideas about how to tackle problems.

The arranged marriage or marriage of convenience are common themes in historical romances, as are mistaken identity or masquerades. Initial distrust or antagonism, in a romance, will gradually change to real love.

There may be conflict arising more from the plot, such as split loyalties, desire for revenge, secrets someone is unable or unwilling to reveal, an enemy from the past or jealousy. It may arise out of rivalry, where only one character can be successful. The idea of a quest fits the historical format well.

Whatever the reason for the conflict, it must be a real one, and matter to the characters. Readers need to care about the outcome, and this must be believable, not contrived.

Tell the reader

Readers need to know the specific goals of each character, what the opposition is, where the conflict arises and how the characters achieve their goals or find a successful compromise, and how each character reacts to success and failure.

Showing readers what the goals are can help to bring scenes alive, make the reader understand the motives. In addition to the major objective there will be intermediate and often small goals, and extra, minor obstacles to a final resolution. The reader doesn't have to know exactly what these are, but the characters must know their own immediate goals so that their behaviour conforms to their efforts to achieve them.

Working out what the goals are can help you form your plot, perhaps by working backwards from the ultimate goal and seeing the necessary steps towards it. You can introduce further complications and comparisons by contrasting the goals of minor characters with those of your protagonists.

Sometimes these can highlight specific characteristics and goals of others, or provide a twist.

Provide a twist

If you analyse books for conflict you will see how often familiar themes are used, but don't be discouraged. One of a novelist's skills is that of taking an old theme and giving it a new look, a twist, a fresh angle.

You needn't confine yourself to one cause of conflict. They can be combined, with several in one book, a variety of minor and major ones for the protagonists, and others in sub-plots.

The action

Keep your characters on the move, doing things. This does not necessarily mean physical activity, but you need plenty of action, physical and emotional. We will look at how to maintain the pace and suspense and tension later on, but for every scene you write, ask the purpose. Why is it there? What does it do? Does it move on the plot or demonstrate some important characteristic?

The writing

Finally, you need good writing. This includes the basics of good spelling and grammar, clarity of expression and appropriate choice of language. It needs more – vivid imagery, telling descriptions, and selective and accurate detail which add to the effect you are trying to create, whether this is emotional or a better understanding of the conditions in which your historical characters live.

Move on from the beginning

You have to provide or promise much of this in the first few pages. Then you have to keep it up throughout the novel. In mainsteam novels you may concentrate on one character to begin with, normally but not necessarily the hero or heroine but you still have to make her (or him) and her (or his) situation so intriguing and compelling, with the same sort of hints and hooks that promise a great read, that the reader reads on.

Try to have something in every scene which moves on the story or develops the characters. This can be conflict, tension, suspense, drama and emotion, as well as the more obvious physical action.

Intrigue the reader

In the beginning, concentrate on main and not minor characters. Start with drama and action, and an emotional tug, something which instantly evokes the reader's sympathy with the main character's situation and the motivation for changing it. You need, in as short a space as possible, to make the story understandable and explain to readers who people are and what is happening, but at the same time not overburden the reader with so much information they can't remember it.

This requires a fine balance between revealing enough to be enticing but not so much that it's stodgy, just enough to lure on readers who can understand the predicament but not foresee the solution.

Don't get bogged down

The opening few pages are the most important part of your book and you'll probably spend as much time on them as on the rest. Don't spend so long at the start rewriting Chapter One that you never reach Chapter Two. You can always come back to it and many writers do the beginning last.

Finish the book, even if you are far from satisfied with your opening. What you learn about your characters as you go on, incidents you may not have thought of before you got to them, twists and surprises which occur to you later, can all indicate how those vital first few paragraphs ought to be written.

Is your plot feasible for the time it's set?

This seems an obvious question, but it is one worth asking. Some plots will only work in a contemporary setting. It isn't just the background matters such as technology – a plot about computer fraud, for instance – it also covers the realistic use of aims and conflicts, and the social conventions which may be different from those in past times.

Knowing what questions to ask

You need to be aware, always, whether what you ask of your characters is feasible and whether it fits in with the attitudes and conventions of their time. Could they, and would they, have done it?

Always ask whether your characters, belonging to a specific class and time, can physically do what you want them to do.

Do they travel?

Can people go where you want them to go? There are the obvious restrictions, such as where women might not be allowed, but at various times and in different societies men and women could not be seen together in certain situations. There were other constraints. Coachmen could not leave the horses to ring a doorbell – you cannot leave horses to their own devices!

In many medieval crime books monks and nuns are the detectives, but they have to have unusual reasons for leaving the cloister. Brother Cadfael was not restricted to the abbey as were many monks, but he had to have good reasons for his journeys into Shrewsbury and beyond, and sometimes special permissions and missions.

Are the roads and bridges, routes and means of transport there? At what times could people travel and what facilities could they expect to be available? Some post houses were accustomed to travellers arriving at all hours and had night ostlers to attend to them.

How do they communicate?

Can your characters read and write and therefore exchange letters? How long would it take a letter to get there? Do they have to employ scribes or pass on messages in some way other than writing? What do they write on and with? Consider the restrictions of stylus and wax, quills and parchment or scrolls and seals. Consider when envelopes and fountain pens and the postal system began.

News could only travel at the speed of a ship or a horse, later of the railways or cars, and even after the invention of radio and TV not everyone possessed these marvels.

How much do they know?

Ask whether they could or would be likely to know about events, inventions, scientific discoveries or technical progress. And if they did know about new inventions, would they have the knowledge or education to understand complications or appreciate their significance?

What about weapons?

What sort of weapons are available and what sort of complications might there be? For example, pistols gave only one shot, revolvers several. When guns had to be prepared with powder before firing, there could be problems if the powder got wet.

Everyday life

Consider domestic or agricultural implements. What was available and what were the methods of cooking? How did they turn a spit? When was baking possible? How was the land cultivated and the food grown? How was food preserved?

What materials were articles made from at different times? Eating implements have changed a great deal, from horn beakers, wooden spoons and trenchers, pewter mugs and plates, two-pronged forks and so on.

Whenever characters are required to perform some action, make sure it comes within the possibilities of their world and experience and they do it according to the conditions and materials available.

What of social restrictions?

These can be very important, for instance in determining how your characters can meet, whom they can meet, where and in what circumstances, and very importantly, whom they might marry.

Are unmarried girls or married women, in various classes, allowed to go out on their own?

Love and marriage

People had shorter life expectancies, so what effect did this have on their attitudes and hopes? Where property and the continuation of the male family line were involved, there could be pressures to marry and produce heirs as early as possible and most people would work as long as they could, until death or physical frailty intervened. They might never get to 'retirement age' or be able to afford to retire when they were old.

Until comparatively recently marriage for love was rare, particularly amongst the landed classes. Marriage to unite estates or for some other advantage was normal. Marriage was still expected if at all feasible but some difficult girls could cause their parents distress if they were unable to attract suitors.

Attitudes towards others

How do people behave towards others – men and women, parents and children, servants and masters?

What are the social rewards or sanctions or the official punishments for transgressions of the law or unwritten codes?

Check that your characters conform to the practices and mores of the times, unless they have extremely potent reasons for disregarding them.

Plotting against the times

There are various reasons for selecting a particular time for the setting of your novel.

Using real events

The plot, with a background of a particular event such as a battle, may determine a novel's period very precisely. Then it is necessary to explain the background, not as in a history lesson, but as the people of the time would view it.

My novel *Runaway Hill* takes place during the Civil War, and was the mocking title given at the time to the Battle of Roundway Down. One character explains.

> *'When the battle was over, they tried to run away, most of 'em, and came right past us, making for Chippenham way. But the hill was steeper than they thought, and many of the horses fell, and rolled down the slopes, over and over.'*

Another, *Petronella's Waterloo*, has obvious connections. The background is explained very plainly towards the end when Napoleon is approaching Paris.

> *'Incredulity changed to panic, and by the middle of March many visitors, including the Duchess of Wellington, were leaving for home, or for the more secure towns of the Low Countries, behind the defensive lines of fortresses that, it was hoped, would keep the former ruler of most of Europe penned in France.'*

Historical themes – universal

You may have a universal theme, such as the generation conflict, which can arise at any time or place but which will be constrained by contemporary beliefs and attitudes, such as respect for elders, dependence on family for financial support or having to make one's own way as soon as possible.

For example, take occupations. A common theme is the need for a girl who did not marry to earn her own living, but the options varied at different times. Now the possibilities are endless, but in the early nineteenth century educated girls from genteel families could do little apart from become companions or governesses. Only the occasional rebel would go onto the stage or open her own milliner's shop. The stage and trade were not respectable. Before Florence Nightingale nurses were despised. To undertake these occupations would exclude her from her own class and the chances of regaining that class would be remote.

Uneducated working-class girls had far more opportunities, from working in the mills, on farms, in shops or domestic service, and there are many examples of fictional heroines, such as Emma Harte in *A Woman of Substance*, who rise to great heights from such beginnings.

Men had more options, but if a man 'of independent means' is disinherited or suddenly loses his fortune, how could he make a living and what effect might it have on his standing within society? Would he still move in the same circles, keep his friends and receive the same deference from former servants or tenants?

Historical themes – applicable at many different times

Your theme may be religious or other forms of intolerance, which gives you the choice of several potential times and places in which to set your story.

Charms of a Witch dealt with the witch-hunting fever during the 1640s.

'She accused Lucy of witchcraft.'

'On what grounds?'

'The accusers of witches do not have to have grounds,' he replied. ' 'Tis enough to say one's cattle have died, someone is ill of a wasting sickness, an unexplained or sudden death, people have lost things...Normal evidence is not possible, since witches are held to work in secret, and invisibly, therefore abnormal evidence is accepted, such as would be laughed at in any other trial.'

Historical themes – applicable at one specific time

You may wish to write a novel with a theme which can be dealt with most appropriately at one particular period – women's suffrage in England, for example.

Player's Wench dealt with the Restoration theatre and the first women to act in public theatres, a controversial action in a time when Puritans were strong and drama itself condemned by them. One character expresses his opinion.

'Plays are an abomination, but to have women who are no better than painted whores flaunting themselves before the rakes of the Court in breeches is an insult to all decent women! It should not be allowed, and if sober citizens had the ear of the King instead of riotous, unprincipled courtiers, it would be forbidden. I wish to hear no more of plays or players from any of you! Go to your rooms, and beg pardon for your wickednesses!'

Following movements

Unlike events, to which you can assign a particular time and place, movements tended to grow slowly and spread to different parts of a country, or to different countries, at variable rates. Think of popular political movements, any rebellion by a ruler's subjects, religious changes, agrarian and industrial revolutions, and try to imagine how they would start.

For most such movements, there would be gradual but increasing mutterings of discontent, writings, or experiments and small improvements. These would spread very gradually until there was considerable pressure for changes. In many cases there would be some catalyst that would draw people together into action or cause a ruler to take some major step, but the underlying demand for such actions had to be present for it to be acceptable. Many novels have followed the fortunes of reformers and rebels, showing the problems faced by all of them. This is an excellent source of conflict.

Resolutions

The manner in which your story is resolved, the conflicts of aims or irreconcilable motives finally decided, will differ in different centuries.

In crime novels especially, the methods of detection will be different. You need to know what sort of official police authorities there are, the forensic possibilities, the contemporary knowledge of poisons, and whether autopsies were advanced enough to detect the causes of certain types of deaths.

Use the differences positively

It is your skill at making your characters and plots, situations and backgrounds, peculiar to the time that will contribute to the success of your novel. Characters must behave, convincingly, of their time.

It's a useful exercise to take a story, perhaps one you have written or the synopsis of one you plan to write, and deliberately set it one or two centuries earlier or later. What would you have to change? As well as events and background details such as dress and communications, how would the non-physical details have to be changed?

Finding ideas

This generally comes in two stages. There is the initial or overall idea of the plot, which can arise from a small incident, a theme, a background or a character you have invented. Then there are the intermediate incidents, which provide your characters with a succession of problems to overcome before the satisfying ending.

Examples of initial ideas

The original idea for *Sibylla and the Privateer* came from reading a paragraph in a guide book on Brittany which mentioned the privateers who hid their boats in some of the coves during the seventeenth century. This gave me a time and place. So I invented a privateer for my hero who journeys across the English Channel smuggling help and information to the Royalists in the Civil War.

Charms of a Witch arose from reading about the witch hunters of the 1640s and their seemingly unrestricted power over others. The heroine is caught up in this process and has to fight to try to escape. This is a plot specific to the time.

Runaway Hill, as described earlier in this chapter, came about because of a battle which had that nickname. This is a specific event. The hero and heroine are involved in this battle.

The Cobweb Cage began from considering the conflicting needs of different members of the same family and how they might be irreconcilable. It's a theme of family loyalties.

The Glowing Hours features gradually increasing skill and ambition and how three girls deal with it in their different ways. Coming from very different backgrounds, but all with problems connected with their families, dancing brings them together and affects their lives. Here there is the theme of attempting to escape from problem families and a background of the musical theatre in the 1930s.

Intermediate ideas

Whatever the type of book you write, whether it's a romance or crime or a western, the path must not be too smooth for your protagonists. If it is you haven't a story. So within the overall idea you need many problems, large and small, which have to be overcome.

You can find suggestions for appropriate difficulties as you read about the times, see what problems real people had then and how they overcame them. But try not to be too slavish, only copying real events. Use your imagination in order to make the difficulties different, more interesting and more complicated.

Working on ideas

When your novel takes hold of your mind, you will find yourself thinking about it during all waking hours when you have no other urgent matters to deal with, like your paid work. Maybe you'll think about it then and even dream about it. Very often ideas will expand, you will think of new twists or find solutions.

Writers find different ways of letting this subconscious process work for them. Going for a walk, doing housework, listening to music, reading a book on a completely different topic, writing letters – anything can be used to help, and the ideas will, if they are valid ones, fall into place.

Posing and overcoming problems

Sometimes a problem encountered will be dealt with straight away, but more often it will be left until later, and even further complications introduced, before it is overcome. This is an important part of the creation of suspense.

A novel is like a fairground roller coaster. Just as your protagonist overcomes one obstacle, and before his life becomes steady and uneventful, another problem looms. As well as ups and downs, life changes direction unexpectedly. Sometimes more than one problem looms at the same time.

Vary the obstacles

There is no rule about the order and intensity of the obstacles, but vary them and try to find a huge one for the final climax. Each predicament should differ in size and complexity, small intermingled with large ones. Try not to have your protagonists (and your reader) overwhelmed by too many at once but don't let too long a time go by before introducing another one. Don't start with the biggest so that, the protagonist having conquered that one, every subsequent battle seems trite in comparison. Finish with an apparently unsurmountable one but not always the most formidable. Make the solution unexpected but convincing.

Overcoming plotting problems

Much the same process of doing something entirely different, to allow ideas to sort themselves out, can be used when you hit a problem in the writing, such as where to go next, though you may have to make a more conscious effort. Perhaps you have a character in a seemingly impossible situation. Either you find a way out or you have to backtrack and avoid the situation. This is where your ingenuity is tested.

In both situations keep on asking 'What if?' What would happen if he or she did this, or that or the other? What would be the most likely decision your particular character, in specific circumstances, would make? At some point you will find a way through the problem.

If it's a different sort of problem, such as not knowing the historical facts or whether what you want to do is practicable, you will have to do more research, and we'll be looking at this later on. You must decide whether to leave the research until later or whether the facts when you have found them must have a crucial influence on your plot. If the latter, you need to stop and find out before you go too far ahead.

Characters have problems

These must be big, they matter, are important, not solved easily and be unexpected, with twists and turns. Don't make life easy for the protagonists or your readers will lose interest. As one problem seems to be on the edge of being resolved, complicate it, add another, increase the intensity. Readers know that in most books, apart from tragedy, a satisfactory ending will be achieved. But try to keep them guessing, don't indicate the obvious, easy solution. Every good book has many moments of suspense.

Even in genre fiction, a romance where readers know the hero and heroine will eventually come together, they need to know how this will happen, how they will overcome their problems, just why and when they admit to themselves and each other that they are in love. Readers know that the murder in a crime novel will be solved, but they want to know how.

There can be a major problem but there will be minor ones along the way to add depth and complexity to your plot. Your protagonists will start off with one major objective but they will have other, small ones as well. Perhaps these will be part of the main one or they may be connected with a subplot.

Suppose someone needs to go on a journey, this is the main objective. To do this they have to find someone to look after people left behind or find a means of conveyance. They achieve these aims, obtain a horse and the horse is lamed. They need another one. Then perhaps they are attacked, injured or have their belongings stolen. This gives them extra problems.

As a sub-plot, perhaps another character does something which distracts the protagonists from the course they are set on, and they have to put aside their own concerns to solve this problem. A young sister elopes and has to be pursued. A baggage waggon is captured so the army have to wait for more supplies or divert from their chosen route to go and obtain them. Or they have to fight whoever has the waggon.

Keep your characters active, doing things, but always facing obstacles and having to overcome them. Unless you can devise enough of these, you are unlikely to have sufficient material for your plot.

Controlling the action

Pace is one way of controlling the action, though to some extent the action determines the pace. The author instigates the events, the action, and then has the task of drawing the reader along, going faster or more slowly according to what he most wants to emphasise. If the author is speeding towards a resolution, the pace can be fast as we approach the brink, with slower sections to dwell on the doubts or dangers. Throughout a book writers must encourage the reader to continue by setting out lures, enticements or hooks. Once caught, like a fish, the reader cannot escape.

Keeping up the pace

To increase the pace you need action, lots of incident, fast dialogue and not too many details which get in the way of the action. Until now the details and the historical accuracy have been stressed, and they are vital, but don't be misled into including everything you have found out whether you actually need it or not. Slip in the essential details as integral parts of the story. That way the readers will absorb them effortlessly. If you introduce superfluous details in a clumsy manner it will destroy the illusion you are creating of a different world.

You need changes of pace throughout, which keep the reader interested. Too much excitement is as boring, in the end, as too little. Vary scenes depending on what you want them to achieve. Important action scenes are fast and exciting. Short sentences increase the pace. Other important scenes, where you want the reader to savour details, can be slow to achieve the required effect.

Description, whether this is of scenery, places or new characters, slows the pace and readers can't remember it all at once. Reflection slows the pace, while rapid dialogue speeds it up.

Dropping hints neatly

You can slide in vital information in many indirect ways. Since the action arises from the characters, by dramatising the characters you can have them demonstrating the essential information and giving hints. Ask what the characters want, what they feel, all the time.

You can show, through concentration on specific details and action, what is important or relevant. This can also be shown by the reactions and comments of other characters. Thoughts may be different from what the outer appearance indicates so use contrast and comparison.

Don't give too much information too soon – only when it's vital to the story. On the other hand don't hold back essential information so that it's anticlimactic. Writers soon develop a feel for what is right at any one time.

Page-turning qualities

Readers want to know what happens, and there are many ways you can delay revealing all so that they go on reading. You can end scenes within chapters or have some break in a scene, such as an interruption or the development of a different strand of argument, which delays the explanation. You can give a hint that some information is about to be revealed. You might introduce uncertainty, so that the reader is led to believe it's the opposite of what she wants to hear, but you must be fair to the reader. As in crime novels, all the clues must be there for the reader but disguised or misleading. You can give a hint of romance, or help to further or destroy it. You can introduce the next obstacle.

Above all, keep readers guessing

Show any danger or threat soon and the strength of it. Where there is a real villain, he must be present early on. If there is any doubt about who the real villain is, as with crime novels with more than one suspect, provide at least two potential villains.

Bury clues in the middle of something exciting, perhaps dramatic action or in dialogue about something else. Have lots of twists, and sudden glimpses of full or partial understanding.

Reveal a character as different from what the reader has so far understood but make sure it is compatible with what has been shown before or there is a potent reason for any change.

Create more mystery, devising situations in which immediate action is necessary. Introduce new threatening situations. Use an unexpected, unanticipated discovery which puts the character in even more danger.

Create an alarm which turns out to be false and lulls suspicion, then use the same device again for real. There could be a threatened kidnap, which does not happen, then, when people have relaxed, a real one.

Show the villain killing or threatening someone else to prove he's capable of it if he captures a protagonist. Have a rescue which either fails or proves to be a mistake, perhaps leading to increased peril. Have the villain aware that the protagonist knows the truth or can expose him, which will put her in greater danger.

Use objects and imagery which enhance the emotions you want emphasised. Having a time limit always increases the tension.

Above all, avoid coincidences, especially to resolve a climax. This is the easy, lazy way out and editors hate them.

Cliffhanging techniques

Although these usually come at the ends of chapters, you should use them throughout – at the ends of scenes, in the middle of scenes – with the most effective ones at the chapter ends. Not every chapter does finish with a cliffhanger in the regular sense, but there will always be unfinished business or questions to which the reader needs answers. A few examples follow.

John appeared to hesitate; half-turned as if to try and regain the platform; then hurled Ivy away from him on to the other track. He turned again, but by now the front of the train was towering above him. He leapt after Ivy, but the engine caught him a glancing blow. As he fell, the great iron horse drew to a shrieking halt and hid everything from the watching crowd. (*The Cobweb Cage*)

Nell heard the bones snap as Frank fell. With a sob she flung herself down beside him and touched his face. Then she shuddered as Frank's head, his neck broken, lolled helplessly away from her. By the time she absorbed this and looked up, she was alone with his body. *The Glowing Hours*

She could even begin to save a few pennies each week, and by their unaided efforts she and her mother might get out of this slum. It might take years, but they would do it.

Then, in the height of summer, Dora became really ill. (*The Golden Road*)

'You'll pay for that, you little vixen,' he threatened, and Josie, with agonising stabs of pain shooting up from her twisted ankle, her head reeling from where she'd hit it on the door jamb, desperately tried to fight him off. (*The Golden Road*)

When he (the landlord of an inn) had disappeared, Ludovick turned back to the door. He did not knock, but coolly lifted the latch and walked in. *Campaign for a Bride*

As he finished, from the village in front of them a line of men filed through the gateway and stood, guns raised, aiming at the returning group. (*Forbidden Love*)

Chapter endings

You can finish at the conclusion of some event or in the middle of it. Whatever you do, try to end each chapter on a note which makes the reader surprised, smile or wonder. These devices build suspense and pull the reader along.

You can have something which affects a character's spirit, a low or a high point in their lives, a calamity or a success. Provide a surprise with a flash of action, some insight or revelation. Pose a question, to which the answer will be given in the next chapter. Have a decision taken but don't reveal what it is. Issue an ultimatum.

All these devices cause the reader to want to move on to the next chapter, to find out what happens next.

Relishing scenes

You should enjoy the scenes you create as much as readers do, both from the pride in achievement and because they are good.

Increasing the tension

You can keep up the enjoyable excitement by changing the mood, introducing new and portentous elements, creating more mystery, showing characters in new and different lights and devising situations in which immediate action is necessary.

Do your characters always behave realistically for their time?

Have you included enough events and details which add to or enhance or explain your story and set it more firmly in the historical context? If not go through your notes to find more ideas.

Make sure you have not included details, events or references just for the sake of it. Check that everything is relevant to your plot and adds to the atmosphere without being intrusive or superfluous.

Begin making notes of queries, things you need to check or research to make sure your details are accurate.

Hooks

Hooks are very similar to cliffhangers, and your first paragraph, sentence and page must lure the reader on. They can also be employed at the ends of chapters, but they are used prolifically all the way through. Every question which has to be answered, every surprise, every new fact revealed, every change which is forecast, every disaster, every complication or obstacle which prevents characters from achieving their goals, are hooks.

Don't explain everything or answer every question too soon. Provide the reader with suspense making her eager to turn the page to discover what is going to happen.

'Nell, my dear,' he said, 'I'd give anything not to have to tell you this. It's bad news.' (The Glowing Hours)

Caro watched in frustration. The mounted man had an almost unbreakable advantage over them both, with Robert on foot and her only remaining weapon, the small dagger, thrust into her boot. There would be no time to get Robert mounted on her horse, so somehow she had to try and unseat the robber. But how could she achieve that? (Her Captive Cavalier)

Each step became a gigantic struggle, and he was sinking past his knees. He felt his boots dragged off him, and for a few steps the going was easier, but soon he was unable to lift his feet high enough to clear the ground and take another step forward. He began desperately to pray. (Sibylla and the Privateer)

He turned, smiled blandly at Mrs Deeping and Amarylis, who had followed them up the stairs, and left the room. Petra, striving to stifle her giggles at their perplexed expressions, resigned herself to the inevitable questions, reproaches, and exclamations that were about to break around her. (Petronella's Waterloo)

Can you find a satisfying ending?

Agents, editors and readers want to be able to put a book down with a sigh of satisfaction.

In some literary novels the outcome is hinted at rather than explained and can be downbeat. In most other novels endings tend to be upbeat and it's more satisfying for the reader to know what happened. Did the hero get the girl, the detective unmask the crook, the explorer return safely or the soldiers win the battle? How were these resolutions finally concluded?

Make certain all the ends you want to tie up are satisfactorily explained and you haven't overlooked some vital piece of evidence in your relief at finishing.

A satisfying ending is not necessarily a happy one, but it must be logical and follow from what has gone before. You can connect the ending to the beginning with some allusion or repetition, but most endings reach a climax where the protagonists achieve some ambition and get what the reader feels they deserve after all their trials and endeavours.

Before you give your protagonists their ending, clear up all the other strands and sub-plots, tuck them in and get the other characters off-stage. Leave the stage clear for this final scene and make it a scene – action rather than discussion, including essential explanation within it.

Questions to answer and things to do

1. Make a list of the conflicts in the novel. Do you have both internal and external? Are they between protagonists, and also between protagonists and major characters?
2. Which are the three most important scenes in your novel, and where do they occur? They are probably near the beginning, right at the end and somewhere in the middle.
3. How many sub-plots do you have, what is the purpose of each and are they all essential? Do they add to the main plot – by contrasting with it, mirroring it or helping to resolve it?
4. Make lists and add to them as you think of other examples, of appropriate aims any of your characters might have in the time in which your novel is set. Are these the main ones, but also perhaps some minor ones?
5. Make a second list of possible areas of conflict, not simply for your main characters, but for minor ones too. Two minor characters might have some kind of rivalry which could affect what they do and thereby determine what their influence on events might be.

6. Make notes for the future. These could be notes for incidents or characters you will find useful in this novel or ideas for the next one. As you read and do research many ideas will occur to you. Make a list of themes and say at which historical periods they might be most appropriately used.

Tips by example

For my second example, and assuming that Marion is the most important protagonist, the first major scene might be where she defies her father and determines to get a job. Halfway through there could be a turning point where her father is dying, she has discovered that his wartime activities were in fact illegal and she has to decide whether to tell her mother and brother that their inheritance is tainted. The final major scene would be, since this is a romantic novel, where she and the man she chooses finally commit themselves.

The other two girls would have sub-plots and similar major scenes.

Key points

1. Middles sort out good from average novels.
2. Have major crises spread out and small ones in between.
3. Take care with sub-plots.
4. You need a strong enough plot.
5. You need lots of conflict.
6. Characters need aims and motives.
7. Intrigue the reader.
8. Ensure the plot is feasible for the time it is set.
9. Ask questions and check all the facts.
10. Make resolutions plausible.
11. Work on ideas.
12. Give characters problems.
13. Control the action and pace.
14. Use cliffhangers and hooks.
15. Make the ending satisfying.

7 Convincing settings

Paying attention to detail

This relates to research and to the accuracy and note-keeping which is necessary. Detail is important for adding reality, but don't force it.

You need to use a variety of techniques, interesting characters, a strong plot, combining historical detail with imagination, and many more, to make a successful novel. Use plenty of appropriate, specific detail to illustrate your novel, not generalisations, but don't pile it on too lavishly.

Don't overdo or repeat anything too much. If repetition is important for a special reason, if the weather is important to your story or is needed to mirror moods, for example, find different ways of mentioning the weather, bringing in references or allusions. Characters are wet or cold, rain can be lashing the windows or a journey takes longer because of a snowstorm.

If your novel is, in whole or part, a love story, there will be plenty of emotion. A different kind of emotion will be necessary in war and adventure stories.

Be accurate

Do your very best to get all your facts right. If you don't someone will notice and they'll lose faith in the rest of your story and probably lose interest too. Check absolutely everything, even the things you think you know. If you make a mistake you immediately lose your reader who will not trust anything else you tell him.

It is the small, simple fact that you think you know, or don't even consider needs to be researched, that is most likely to let you down. Do your research, and take the advice given to all writers – if you can't find out the fact you need to know, leave it out. There is usually some way of dealing with the scene to get round this.

Check invented facts too

As well as making sure all the real detail is accurate, keep notes on details you have invented. This can include background facts which belong to the character profiles, but which you may not have thought of to begin with, such as additional family members, a reference to a childhood illness or accident, what they do as the story progresses, what information they have about others or their beliefs and attitudes. Make notes as you go or when re-reading your work.

Record permanent details, such as colours of eyes and hair and other physical details in character profiles, to remind yourself when necessary. If there is a long timescale, keep track of the ages and make sure all the characters age by the same amount.

When any information is revealed, especially if this is a crime novel, make a note, and also include which characters already know the facts or when they learn them, so that you don't have someone acting on the basis of something he couldn't have known.

Keep track of the time of day, the days of the week and the passing seasons. Make sure the right flowers are blooming or the correct farm work is being done. In some books it feels as though there are a hundred hours in a single day. If you have characters doing a lot, make sure it's physically possible for them to fit it into the time. Can they travel that distance, for example? Similarly don't let a pregnancy continue for two years. This all sounds very obvious, but in the excitement of the writing it's easy to overlook.

Details of places

Try if at all possible to visit any real places you use for background. They will have changed over the centuries, even over the decades, but seeing old buildings, the street pattern of towns or the basic geography of a place – the hills and valleys, rivers and roads – which may not have changed, can give you a proper feeling about the location and an instinct for what will work or not.

If your story is set in the past, get a map as close as possible to the time of the story. Get large-scale maps, and for more recent times check one-way streets and pedestrian precincts, the location of public buildings and hotels, and whether these existed at the time of your novel.

When I was researching the Monte Carlo Rally for *The Golden Road*, I knew the name of the hotel where the British teams had stayed in Monaco that year, but it was no longer in any gazetteer. I eventually found it on an old photograph in a small museum, and discovered it was still there but had been converted into a post office and apartments. I was able to see inside the ground floor, which still retained elaborate corridors and marble pillars, so was able to add details of what my characters saw.

If your characters look out of a window at a distant range of hills, make sure it's possible to see them. Check they could, at the appropriate date, catch trains or ferries to wherever they were going. Then check the time it would have taken them to travel by whatever form of transport was used. If you guess wrongly, someone will know.

Details of clothes and other possessions

Use clothes and other possessions to add to what we know about the characters. They must be realistic. If your hero is wealthy he may have a good horse and a smart carriage, unlike the poor villager who may only have a broken-down nag and not even a rough cart. Only rich knights could afford full armour. Rich women would have several gowns, a poor girl maybe only one. Poor people might very rarely eat meat. Consider what your characters could afford and what priorities they would have had, given their income or other assets such as a garden in which to grow food or keep poultry.

See people through the eyes of characters

Each scene will be from a character's viewpoint, a technique we'll look at later. When you describe a character, try to do this by showing them as someone else sees them. This can be useful not just for the main purpose of letting your reader know what they look like, but also how the other character regards them.

A girl might be described as pretty with Titian hair by someone who admires her. A jealous rival might say she looks coarse and too bold with that mop of carroty hair. The clothes we wear often indicate our characters. If someone always wears red or black, ask why? If they are always immaculate, or always scruffy, what does it tell us about them? Describing your characters' clothes helps readers to visualise them and know them better. But be careful, too much detail may be irrelevant and hold up the story. A couple of pertinent facts will bring an image to mind but superfluous detail will be overwhelming.

See places through the eyes of characters

This tells us about the characters as well as whatever they are describing. People vary in their reactions to things. The practical ones, on seeing an ancient castle, would think at once of the cost of upkeep and perhaps of the income that could be obtained by admitting the public. Others, more likely to be historical novelists, would imagine its past glory. If you are a crime novelist you might be more inclined to think of any sinister aspects, and if you have no feel for history you might consider it an eyesore.

Similarly the castle will mean different things to different characters. To one it may mean home. To a new bride it will mean her future home, and she may look forward to this or not. To an enemy it means a place where he is to be imprisoned. To a servant it may be his place of work, where the work is hard and menial or he is frequently beaten. To local villagers it offers protection but to an invading army an obstacle they need to overcome. Show this by how they react to it.

Make sure there are not too many details

Ask if there is enough or too much detail, and if they are the right ones to add to the story. Scatter facts a few at a time, where they fit in with the story. Make characters ask for or seek out facts, not just tell each other without being asked. And try to avoid telling readers the facts from the author's viewpoint.

For instance in *The Cobweb Cage*, Marigold overhears two men discussing the latest news.

> *'Those damned Serbs are at it again'*
> *'What's that? Serbs?'*
> *'Don't think the damned Balkans will ever get sorted out. They're like Ireland, always a problem. Some fanatic shot an Austrian Archduke. Place called Sarajevo, or something like that. Ever heard of it?'*

Make description integral

Whatever details you choose to include, they should be part of the story. By this I mean important in the plot, or setting the mood or showing us what a character is feeling. It should help the reader experience the story and it should not be just for decoration. Slip in descriptions where they are appropriate and not as separate chunks which break the pace and flow of the narrative.

At the beginning of *The Cobweb Cage* the young Marigold is cold, and contributing to this is the fact that *The chenille curtain was caught up on a nail instead of falling over the door, and a bitter cold draught whistled through from the scullery.* This explains part of the cause of her distress but also illustrates an item of furnishing common at that time.

Again in *The Cobweb Cage*, there is a tiny reference to a weather statistic, using it as part of the background.

> *'Phew, it's hot today!' Marigold said as she came in and sat down to her own sewing.*
> *'They do say it's the hottest day ever recorded,' John glanced across at them.*

In *The Golden Road*, on one of the rallies, they go to a local hill called The Beacon. The name and the position are emphasised, but give an opportunity of mentioning technical developments related to signalling.

'On weekdays the smoke is so thick you can't see the few miles to Walsall, let alone beyond Wolverhampton,' Matthew said. 'If they used these hilltops to light beacon fires it might be difficult to see them.'

'No need, now we've got radio and the telephone,' William Scott replied.

Make description unobtrusive

Narrative is a combination of dialogue and description, and the pace is usually faster during dialogue. Readers often skip over long pages of unbroken description, but if the essential facts of description are slipped in as unobtrusively as possible, as part of the action, they are absorbed almost without being noticed. Slide facts into your work and only include those which are important to illustrate your story. Nine-tenths of what you research will be below the surface.

If you want to describe scenery or buildings, do it through the eyes of a character who sees it for the first time or with some powerful emotion such as relief at returning home.

In *Cavalier Courtship*, they reach London.

Caroline stared wonderingly about her at the huge buildings, mostly of wood and plaster, and crowded so close together that often in the alleys there was space enough for nothing wider than a barrow.

Even before they came to the first buildings, Caroline wrinkled up her nose at the smell which greeted them. The stink of refuse of all kinds was on hot days almost unbearable, and Caroline, used to the fresh air of the countryside, was nauseated.

The character who notices that a tree has been cut down and opened up some vista, or wanders round a room touching new and familiar objects can convey succinctly so much more, about himself as well as the surroundings, than an outsider's account, which can read like an inventory.

Accounts of events are much more dramatic if your characters are directly involved. Your story will be most effective if you mix the straightforward description with dialogue and the reactions of characters.

Give hints and suggestions

Often these are far more effective than a simple bald account. Readers can use their own imaginations to fill gaps and they will therefore be more involved in the story. Readers often have more vivid imaginations than can be provided by any verbal description.

This applies especially to scenes of violence and sex. It can be more horrific to focus on surrounding details of normality than describe the physical specifics of an execution. It can be more erotic to suggest sexual tension and fulfilment than go into minute clinical detail, which inevitably becomes repetitive.

Some writers are happy to include graphic details of violence but if you don't enjoy it there is no compulsion to do it. It can sometimes be more effective to suggest or provide a single horrid detail.

Show, don't tell

This is advice frequently given to aspiring writers. Quite simply, showing means getting inside your characters and presenting the action and emotion as they experience it. It involves devising scenes.

Telling is narrating from outside, as if you are the audience looking down on a stage, experiencing everything at second, not first, hand. There are times when a little discreet telling is necessary – briefer and better than an awkward, contrived scene which lasts for only half a dozen swift exchanges.

Exposition

This is a type of description when an explanation is necessary. The writer breaks away from the scene to give the background, some essential information or a summary of events leading up to it.

It slows the action and is distancing. Readers will be interested only if they feel it is relevant and want to know. As with other description it can be more effective if built into the action, but sometimes it would be false if characters amicably discuss something they know perfectly well, like who inherited Aunt Dottie's money. If they are the right sort of people, and it fits your story, you could convey this information by having them row about it. Or they could explain it to a stranger, but only if he has some interest. If these devices are not possible it may have to be simple telling.

Show things happening

Make them part of the main action and use them to add excitement and incident to your story. In *The Golden Road*, the imaginary characters take part in the 1935 Monte Carlo Rally, which is thoroughly documented in biographies and the motoring magazines. Many genuine incidents are brought in.

For example, the imaginary characters have to halt abruptly in dense fog, which causes the heroine to hurt her arm and leads on to a development in the relationship. They walk forward to discover that, '*The front of Healey's car was a mangled wreck, and looming over it was a long train, ghostly faces peering down from dimly-lit windows.*'

Have your characters talk about what happens

Later in the chapter a brief stop-over is used to convey more of the real details, which competitors swap as they ask the imaginary characters about Donald Healey's crash and comment on the competitors who have dropped out and the conditions. These are some sample comments.

> '*Hear about Rupert Riley? His car went over a cliff. Caught on a bush, they were damned lucky to get out -* '
>
> '*I hear they've had three feet of snow and ten degrees of frost near Bucharest. No one will get through from there this year.*'

> '*Whalley's lucky. He ditched the Ford, but Cathcart-Jones and his Lagonda crew pulled them out.*'

Include details unobtrusively

When you do this, make it relate to your characters in some way. In *Campaign for a Bride*, just before the Battle at Powick Bridge outside Worcester, I put this.

> '*Ludovick was up at dawn on the fateful day, September the third, and with several other officers climbed to the top of the Cathedral tower from where they could see the country for miles around.*'

Use all the senses

As with other details, use references to what we experience through our senses to enhance our knowledge of the characters or create a special mood or atmosphere.

The senses most involved will be seeing and hearing, but don't limit yourself to the obvious. Sudden sights of particular things bring back memories, as can hearing a tune or smelling something associated with a previous experience. Use this device to introduce a fact or recollection.

Make the characters active, experiencing things. Show someone stroking velvet or a cat or a rose petal, or choking on dust, or shivering in the snow, rather than just describing the presence of velvet or dust or snow. Whenever you describe something try to see if it could be done more effectively through something a character does.

Sight

If asked to describe a room, what would you be most likely to mention first? The vast majority of people would make a list of what they could see. We all tend to concentrate on the sense of sight but the others may be even more important or vivid in some situations. Shut your eyes, eliminate sight and test what is the next most important sense. The chances are it would be sound, probably followed by smell.

Sight is the dominant sense but it covers far more than the mere appearances of objects. If you were describing fully everything you could see you would need to mention dimensions of the room, the furniture, and the pictures and ornaments. You would say whether the objects of furniture were close together, how big they were in relationship to the room and its shape, and to each other.

It would be important to know whether the lighting was natural, from a sunny exterior, side or ceiling windows, or whether the room was lit by electricity, candles, lamps or firelight, or a combination.

You would probably mention colours, of the furniture, curtains or cushions, but would you comment on the varying shades, or the texture of the wood or plastic, glass or ceramics, oil or watercolour paintings, bindings of books, the fabrics and even the skin or the fur of people or animals inhabiting the room?

It isn't necessary to go into all this detail, which would not be remembered by the reader. You don't need an inventory, but be aware of all the possibilities and try to avoid the obvious. Choose a few effective details which match or contrast with, say, a character's mood, or illustrate something about the owner of the room or the person entering it.

Sound

This is extraordinarily difficult to reproduce using phonetics. Onomatopoeia is the technical name for doing it, and we have a number of familiar words such as hiss or whisper which represent the sound they describe fairly well.

Rather than risk being inaccurate or misunderstood, trying to invent a new word or struggling to describe a sound accurately, it is best to mention the source of the sound and leave the hearing of it to the reader's own imagination. They have heard church bells, alarm clock bells bicycle bells and all are different, not even all bicycle bells are the same.

You could describe the tone, harsh or soothing, whether it is close by, which direction it comes from, and by now the reader will have an excellent impression of the sound, even if it is not quite the same as the one you heard.

Smell

This is as difficult to describe as sound, but most readers will have memories of burnt potatoes, scorched toast, roses, horse manure, honeysuckle and farm fertilisers.

If you need to describe a smell which you think they won't have come across, all you can reasonably do is compare it with some other smell, or even several – it had a sweet sickliness, like the heavy blossom of rapeseed, overlaid by the pungency of vinegar, and below this the throat-catching stench of rotting vegetation – for example.

Smells can be remarkably evocative. A sudden whiff of baking bread could transport your heroine back into her grandmother's farm kitchen, to when she was three years old, parted from her parents for the first time while they go on holiday. She might recall her bewildered loneliness and fear of the cackling farmyard geese or the delights of playing with baby lambs and searching for warm hens' eggs and picking cherries in the orchard. Such associations can provide you with valuable imagery.

Touch

The feel of things is also difficult to convey accurately and is less necessary than the other senses in many stories, but in romantic fiction it can be very important indeed. It's not only the touching of hands, the meeting of lips and deeper intimacies that can be described through the textures felt. The physical and emotional reactions caused through the sense of touch form an important element, in particular in many love scenes.

Taste

It is difficult to describe except through comparison with known, familiar tastes, but can be effective.

Try to make use of any of the senses which can help to establish a mood, or describe a scene or an emotion fully, so that your reader has as full an experience of it as possible.

Find appropriate imagery

It's the creation of mental pictures that allows the reader to experience a story. There is greater reality and fuller participation by the reader when description is accurate and relevant.

Imagery will often help to make a description or emotion more vivid, more precise, but the prime function should be to make clearer what the writer intends. Imagery should serve a purpose, it must not be inserted just for its own sake. It should also be appropriate for the character – a dreamy, artistic girl would not find images from highly technical ideas or a foreign visitor from local history.

Similes

A simile is an imaginative rather than literal comparison. It has to be apposite to add to the reader's perception or understanding of what he is being told. Similes are stated directly, using words 'as' or 'like', and there are dozens of common ones.

They have become clichés because they are overused, but they are used so much because of their aptness and the unwillingness or inability of writers to think of something fresh which is equally effective.

Similes, therefore, may be less valuable to a writer than metaphor. 'She swam like a fish' is a simile.

Metaphors

'She is a fish' is a metaphor, and it is both subtler and more revealing because it has other associations the reader will pick up. Fish are cold-blooded, they are slippery, they wriggle and are difficult to hold. They can be caught through trickery or clever tactics, they fight, the angler can play a fish until it's exhausted and gives up.

A reader won't necessarily think of all these extra connotations, but they can form his subconscious attitude towards the character and possibly towards the other character who regards her as a fish.

Recurring metaphors

You can have a central or recurring metaphor running through the book, but weave it in subtly, don't overdo it. Perhaps you can continue the fishy metaphor by also using references to boats or nets, the sea and rivers. The fishy character might have large eyes, shiny skin, slinky hips and glide along instead of striding.

Don't mix them

You will probably use several different metaphors in your novel at different times, even when you have a central one, but don't mix them. It not only confuses readers, it can destroy the mood you intended to create by inducing unseemly giggles. *'It was no longer a bed of roses when the euphoria vanished and they got down to brass tacks'* sounds painful and unlikely, while *'She was the kind of person who buried her head in the sand while the others were beating the drum'* would probably transport readers to a desert war rather than the offices of a protest organisation.

Your characters can mix metaphors, though, if this is fitting, and it can be very funny if you can devise especially maladroit mixtures. However, don't repeat this device, or any other, too frequently. Don't use very unusual words too often, either. Instead of providing amusing touches or vivid insights they become noticeable and the reader finds them tedious or false or forced.

Questions to answer and things to do

1. Write an opening scene setting out the time and place as early as possible.
2. Do this again using a different method, and decide on the most effective way.
3. Is every fact or historical reference you mention relevant? Check and if not, delete them.
4. Does a reference add to or enhance the scene, or is it intrusive and unnecessary? If it is not essential, delete.

123

5. Have you ever spotted a factual or continuity mistake in a book, or wondered whether something could be the way it was described? If so, how would you rewrite the scene to avoid the mistake?

6. Consider ways in which you can 'show, not tell' your scenes. Will it always work, and if you have to 'tell' can you do it briefly?

7. Do some books sag in the middle? Can you identify the reasons and say how you would have avoided or got round the problems to make the books tauter?

8. Have you included any anachronisms? If so, find other ways of conveying your meaning.

Tips by example

For the Pepys novel, I would try to see all the places Pepys knew which are still there. For others I would try to find pictures, spend time in the National Portrait Gallery looking at the clothing and the background in portraits painted of any people of the time. I would make lists of the sounds and smells common at the time in London, look at pictures of street scenes, and think about imagery connected with the sea, since Pepys became an official of the Navy Board at this time.

Key points

1. Make sure all facts, real or invented, are correct and consistent.
2. Visit the places featured if you possibly can.
3. Use a character's viewpoint to see people and places.
4. Use description and detail sparingly and appropriately.
5. Show, don't tell.
6. Use all the senses.
7. Use appropriate imagery.

8   **Dialogue**

Novels need plenty of dialogue

Dialogue is more effective than any amount of straight exposition, and makes a scene more immediate, as well as speeding it up or creating tension. A popular novel probably contains about two-thirds dialogue to one-third narrative. Most of the short examples in this chapter are from *The Glowing Hours*.

Dialogue should be dramatic. Try to envisage every scene as if it were on a stage where actors need to show everything by what they say or do. What characters do as they speak can add to the meanings or be functional. These may be gestures or actions such as putting on the kettle.

Make the actions appropriate for the emotions of the time. Angry people will speak and behave in a different fashion to frightened ones. Kitty here is obviously furious. *'You are both ungrateful little tarts! Not only do you wake me up, you behave disgracefully with my guests!'* In the next example, Nell is afraid for her little brother. *Nell turned and hastily shoved Benjy up the stairs in front of her. 'Hurry! Yer don't want him beatin' you too!'*

On a stage there can be no thoughts or reflections or flashbacks to explain matters to the audience. Speech and actions, and facial expressions and gestures, have to convey all the information and emotion.

When novels are as close to this as possible, using exposition only when dialogue is inappropriate, or to set or connect scenes, they are livelier and more variable in pace.

Dialogue has many functions

Try to make every single speech perform at least one, and preferably two, of its many functions.

It gives information

In the first place dialogue can be used to provide information in a more direct and interesting way than exposition. People talk to one another, tell each other things, ask questions and get answers. A lot of the back history I warned you against earlier can be introduced by way of conversations.

> 'What happened last night?'
>
> 'I went out for a cigarette. I was being good, dear coz, knowing how you feel about the smell - '
>
> 'Not me; Mama. She's fanatical, and even though she's on the other side of the Atlantic, thank God, and long may she stay there, she'd hear about it from Meggy. And that would be the end of your free room and board here, my sweet.'

It reveals relationships

The words people use, their vocabulary and control of grammar and the way they say things can reveal the characters of both speaker and hearer. Each character should have an individual voice, a way of speaking which is distinctive and recognisable. Nell speaks less broadly than her sisters, and Amy less so than Eth.

> 'Nell, don't leave me!' Amy, lying top to toe between her older sisters, sat up suddenly. 'Tek me with yer, please! I couldn't bear it if yer weren't 'ere!'
>
> 'You're too little, police 'ud send yer back. An' lie down, Amy, yer mekin' it wus!' Eth grumbled. 'It's bloody cold wi'out that shawl. Yer shouldn't a' took it!'
>
> Nell sighed with exasperation. 'I'll go and look fer it tomorrow. I know where I dropped it.'

Ideally, if you have three people talking, readers should be able to tell from their speech which one is speaking.

It shows how people feel

The way they speak to others will also show something about the relationships. Remember that your characters will talk differently to different people. Servants will speak differently to their employers, their fellow workers, and their families or children, if they have them. Your characters' ways of talking to a child, for instance, will not be the same as how they talk to adults, and they might abuse or tease close friends or relatives in a way they wouldn't their boss or a stranger. In the following example, Nell has lost a patch-box, and the exchange shows Kitty's attitude to her maid, Meggy.

'It was in one of the drawers of the chest. It could have slipped under the paper.'

'I don't go grubbing about under drawer linings,' Kitty said with a slight shudder. 'I didn't find it.'

'Meggy might have done. Please, would you ask her to look?'

'If it means so much to you. Though if she did find it, she might not admit it.'

Nell was shocked. 'Meggy would never steal anything,' she said indignantly.

'You have more faith in her than I do,' Kitty drawled.

It shows what characters are like

At the same time, the characters can be showing what they are like by their attitudes, choice of words and so on. They can also be conveying information about their moods, what they and other people have done, how they regard people and events and their intentions or thoughts.

We have seen a couple of examples showing Kitty's character, but she frequently used words such as *simply divine*.

It moves the plot forward

By giving information, making decisions, having arguments, making plans, discovering facts, and in many other ways, dialogue moves on the plot. Gwyneth has been promoted to a more advanced dancing class and is practising hard.

'I must catch up. Mr Bliss is planning to send out a troupe of girls to local theatres soon. I might be good enough to be in it.'

'But what about your job here?'

'I'd have to give that up.'

It shows the mood of the speaker

The words chosen, the way they are said, and any accompanying actions will indicate whether the speaker is angry, afraid, petulant, distressed and so on.

'We've done it! We're proper dancers!' Kitty gasped. 'Nell, who could have imagined it! We're dancing in the same troupe!'

It reveals likes and dislikes, attitudes and beliefs

The manner of speaking to other characters, comments made about characters or their actions or their beliefs can show the speaker's own attitudes very clearly.

'I wants me rights!'
  'What does that mean?'
  'You give me daughter a job at this 'ere prance shop.'
  'Nell teaches at my academy of dance, yes. But I employ her, not you. So what is your business with me?'
  'I wants 'er wages.'

It explains the action

As well as giving information, dialogue can reveal what has happened or what might happen in the future, in certain circumstances. Kitty is learning to drive.

An hour later she steered, somewhat uncertainly, back through the gateway of The Firs.
  'There! Thanks, darling, you can hop down now. I'll go out on my own for a few minutes. I know what to do.'
  'No.'
  'What do you mean?'
  Timothy ran his hands through his already ruffled hair and sighed. 'You aren't safe yet, darling. It was providence you missed the tram in the Hagley Road, and you have to give way to horses. You almost ran down that baker's trap.'

It can create suspense, bring about crises, or solve difficulties

There can be menace, disputes or explanations. Nell, because of her age, needs her father's permission to go to Paris. He comes to her lodgings.

'What's all this I hears about yer goin' ter bleedin' Paris ter sit about on the stage in yer birthday suit?' he shouted. Nell's

heart sank. He would never understand. Before she could reply he started again. 'I'm not 'avin' it, see! I'm goin' ter see that 'orrible pimp what's corruptin' me daughter, an' I'll tell 'im what ter do with 'is dratted dancin' classes...'

...The dream was over. She would not be going to Paris.

It can contradict actions

People do not always say what they mean. There can be ambiguity in the words they use, or hints of sub-plots with broken-off speeches or a change of direction. This can be shown by having a character say something, but his thoughts, actions or expression, if they cannot be seen by the other person, will convey something different. However, his listener will be misled by the words, and this can give rise to misunderstandings or conflict.

In *A Clandestine Affair,* for example, Teresa is arguing with her guardian.

'It does not take five minutes to recognise the person you love,' she declared fiercely.

'How truly you speak,' Sir Ingram agreed amiably, casting a swift glance at Mary.

Dialogue is not ordinary speech

You have to solve an apparent contradiction. It is not ordinary speech with hesitations, repetitions, pauses, interruptions in trains of thought and confused explanations, but it must sound natural. Characters in novels ought not to be completely natural in speaking as we do.

Omit irrelevant chit-chat and lengthy discussions or arrangements concerning actions which will be shown later. Leave out the trivial *'How are you?' 'I'm fine, how are you?'* exchanges and anything else irrelevant which adds nothing and is boring, and delete the ums and ahs and the usual hesitations of normal speech unless it's part of the scene to have a stammering or inarticulate character.

Anyone who has read a transcript of a live broadcast will know how ungrammatical and barely literate it often sounds, and to reproduce this would be very difficult for readers. Make your dialogue interesting. It can be witty, funny or tragic.

Make it sound natural

Dialogue should sound natural with contractions such as It's or I'll, and using appropriate words as spoken, not as written in a learned essay. We all tend to write more formally than we speak.

Read it aloud

Reading your dialogue aloud is the best way to check whether it sounds natural. You could record it onto audiotape and play it back, listening for any stiffness, such as 'I am about to do it', when 'I'll do it' would be more likely for most characters. Of course, an elderly, very pedantic person, especially if in a rage, might say that! Listen for awkward phrases and tongue twisters.

Check that the words used are right for that particular character, in the special circumstances, such as to whom he is speaking, and be aware that people tend to use more formal words and sentence patterns when they write than they do in speech. We choose simpler, different words and tend to use shorter sentences when we talk, compared with writing.

Using vocabulary, slang and dialect

These are particular aspects of dialogue and particularly applicable to historicals. Certain words and expressions are well known and associated with Regencies, especially thieves' cant terms.

Slang gets dated

Unless you want to illustrate that your novel takes place in a particular time or section of society, avoid slang. Be careful with historical slang expressions. Many words have changed their meanings over time and could be misinterpreted by today's readers, so make the meaning clear from the context.

The word gay, for instance, now means homosexual, but early in the last century meant light-hearted and full of fun, yet in the eighteenth century a gay girl meant prostitute.

There are other examples. The word quean meant woman in the eleventh century, then whore in the sixteenth, and in the twentieth, when the spelling changed to queen, an older male homosexual. Jade in the fourteenth century meant a broken-down old horse, but by the sixteenth had become a faithless woman.

Be sure that the people in your novel, given their place in society, would use the particular slang expressions. Men might use slang and profanities, but women, especially in the middle and upper classes, would be unlikely to do so.

Pronunciation and dialect

It's always difficult to decide whether to portray regional, foreign or uneducated speech with phonetic spelling, and apostrophes indicating missing letters. Reading pages and pages of such speech can be very irritating, and it's best to hint at it than try to reproduce it accurately.

It can be effective to use for a very minor character, who does not appear much, such as a landlady in *The Glowing Hours* with a very broad Brummie accent, who objects to the girls practising dances.

> '*Yer'll be dun roight now! Oi'm a'tellin' yow, no more bangin' an' thumpin'. Oi runs a dacent 'ouse, an' Oi'm not 'avin' yow lot in it no more! Out yer goos, next wik, sharpish. An that's me last werd!*'

Amy is a more important character and comes in fairly often. She is less broad.

> '*Ma thought yer'd been killed, went ter the hospitals, Then 'er said yer'd bin sold by summat called white traders. What's them, Nell?*'

A similar problem occurs with dialect and foreign words. Too many hide the meaning from readers unfamiliar with them. A few words, intelligible from the context, are enough to give the flavour of the region or person.

Choose your speech carefully

With historicals you need to avoid obviously modern terms, but also too many archaic ones like prithee and forsooth. Turns of phrase, changing the order of words in a sentence, or different patterns and rhythms of speech can do the job more effectively. This also helps to distinguish foreign characters, where they might speak English but put the words in a different order, such as German verbs being at the end of the sentence.

Make dialogue convincing

Your characters will have special habits, ways of speaking, which will help to make them distinctive. Normally speeches will be short, one thought at a time.

Speech tags

Speakers are identified by tags, 'he said', 'Mary said', 'the doctor said'. The word 'said' is almost invisible, but contrived synonyms such as 'uttered' or 'related' become intrusive. Use alternative words only when they are informative, such as 'muttered' or 'shouted', though even here the manner of speaking should be obvious from the general atmosphere or the actual words said.

Sometimes it is clear from the order or the context who is speaking, but the occasional reminder keeps the reader on track and is essential with more than two speakers.

When there is a conversation between two people, an identifying tag need be employed only occasionally, to keep track of who is speaking. There are other ways of doing this, apart from the different voices. A character can address the other by name. Instead of 'John said', you can give his words and then give him an action. A simple example will demonstrate this.

'I will not do it!' John threw his hat down.
Peter leaned across the table. 'You will, you know.'

As well as identifying who is speaking, the actions of throwing down the hat and leaning across the table show anger and threat.

Modifiers

These can be used in narrative, and the same advice applies – use them sparingly. Instead of a string of adjectives, try to find a more expressive noun. Instead of an adverb to qualify a verb, use more precise verbs.

Inexperienced writers tend to scatter far too many adjectives and adverbs, especially when writing dialogue, probably in the belief that they are explaining things better. Instead they are drawing attention to the habit. Anything which makes the reader look at the stylistic mannerisms of the writer is distracting him from what is happening on the page. The writer is not doing the job properly.

An editor seeing a novel with copious use of verbs and adverbs such as exclaimed excitedly, muttered angrily, shouted furiously, asked curiously, and so on will probably shudder and return the script immediately.

The words spoken should demonstrate how the speaker is feeling. If you explain this afterwards it is too late, the reader will have missed the implication. For example, 'I am going to Australia,' he said – furiously? excitedly? fearfully?

Change it by adding a few relevant words to show the meaning. 'You can do as you like! I'm going to Australia!' he said. Or 'I'm so looking forward to going to Australia,' he said. Or 'How shall I cope? I'm going to Australia,' he said.

Of course, some of these verbs and adverbs, modifying speech, need to be used occasionally. So do adjectives, used appropriately, but restrict your use of them. Use 'said' as the normal speech tag. It's a small word and tends to disappear or be overlooked because the reader does not have to spend time working out what is meant.

Questions to answer and things to do

1. Read your dialogue aloud. Does it sound natural? Are sentences or speeches too long or too convoluted? People talk differently from how they write.
2. Look in contemporary books and make lists of words in use then, which may be archaic now.
3. Write out a conversation with three speakers, making each speaker identifiable without speech tags by their styles of speech or their opinions.

Tips by example

Looking through Pepys' Diary I came across the following words and constructions which are unlikely to be used today.

- No more in family but us three
- she hath them
- doth speak
- went forth
- hath writ
- After all this discourse
- for his pains
- Thence I went
- missed of him
- did of himself think
- is afeared
- he doth much rejoice to see
- failed of finding him
- I had not in the house
- they being just come
- my nose was much swelled with cold
- going thither
- we did discourse
- did eat
- George and I fiddled a good while

Key points

1. Dialogue is crucially important in any novel.
2. It has many functions.
3. It must sound natural but is not.
4. Make slang appropriate and the meaning clear by the context.
5. Beware of too much dialect, which might not be understood.
6. Beware of too much gadzookery (fake historical language), which might not be understood.
7. Make speech tags simple.
8. Beware too many modifiers.

Some other techniques

We have looked at various techniques but sometimes writers have problems or get so involved in the details of their work they cannot see the whole picture.

Overcoming writer's block

There are several versions of this phenomenon, being unable to write, and the solutions depend on the cause.

Many writers, especially journalists who may have many short deadlines and have to produce something each day, say that writer's block simply does not exist. It can be hard to overcome any disinclination to write, but it is possible.

Novelists give many suggestions but mainly advise to keep going, write something, anything, something different, even shopping lists, to get back into the process of writing.

Possible causes and solutions

A traumatic event like a bereavement can halt the creative process. As time passes you will recover. For some people writing can in itself be healing or a therapy.

Inauspicious surroundings can make concentration difficult, but P. G. Wodehouse wrote half a novel with his typewriter perched on a suitcase, in the recreation room of a German internment camp surrounded by 50 men singing and playing games, with armed guards peering over his shoulder. He later wrote a chapter while in a police cell in Paris, and 100 pages in hospital. You too can overcome disadvantages if your writing means enough to you.

Just not feeling in the mood for writing could be laziness, a disinclination to work or have a deeper cause such as not wanting to work on the current project. Overcoming it is up to you and how determined you are to become a writer. Sit down and type (or write) anything. Reply to some letters which have been waiting around, copy some pages from a favourite book or the last few pages you wrote. The act of typing often stimulates ideas and renewed enthusiasm.

Not knowing how to continue often indicates there is something wrong with your novel. It may be from lack of ideas, not knowing your characters well enough, too little plot, not enough or not a big enough conflict or because you have dug yourself into a hole. Reading over what you've done may produce ideas for the next scene. You may need to go back and make changes which will provide the answer.

Analyse what you have written to see whether there is a fault and, if there is, try to put it right. Bring in a new character. Think about the problem before going to sleep and the subconscious may solve it for you.

You may have to abandon the project, at least for the moment. If you do, make sure you start something else right away. This will restore your confidence and keep you in practice.

Do something else

There are always other tasks connected with your writing that can occupy your time until you can get back to the creative part.

You could do some research, read background books, read your notes, make more notes, tidy your notes or reorganise your filing system. Or you could go through your file of new ideas and make plans for future novels. You might even start one and return to the first later. You could catch up on a host of other 'office' tasks which you don't have time for when being creative.

The right facts

Never deviate from the known historical facts. Research all those facts which are important to the accuracy of the story or background. Never assume you know something – always check.

The right way to present them

The information needs to be slipped in unobtrusively. It breaks the flow of a story if you insert a chunk of descriptive narrative for the sole purpose of explaining some facts. If you have your characters baldly telling one another the facts, it usually comes across as very false, an unnatural thing for them to do. You have to make the discovery of the necessary information a part of the action. Either make them ask someone who can answer the questions, or go and find out what they want to know, by looking, reading a book, going to a library or museum.

Sometimes you can have a character who is an expert, and who can therefore explain things naturally. For a very simple example, if your hero has to travel to a particular town and a friend used to live there, the hero can reasonably ask which is the best hotel. But you need to have introduced this expertise some time earlier, not bring it in, very conveniently, when wanted. Establish the experts by showing them in action, talking about the town, so that other characters as well as readers believe they're experts.

Using the research

When you are describing the place you will do it differently depending on which of your characters offers the description and how. Don't describe it like a guide book.

Use your plot. Does your character see it as a tourist who wants to visit all the sites or someone wanting specific information? Is he a longtime resident, who takes things for granted, or a newcomer with practical needs and a fresh look?

Controlling the pace

Pace and rhythm vary from book to book and within one book. Scenes, action and dialogue are more immediate than description. Lots of short sentences, staccato dialogue and urgent action increase the pace. Longer sentences, description and reflection slow it. Quick switches of scenes, lots of cliffhangers, add to the pace and tension.

If the pace is rapid it creates more tension. So does an intensive conflict. Jeopardy is something dire which is being anticipated but it must be a possible outcome, within the conventions of the genre, to make the reader concerned. This adds to the tension, and if there is some sort of time constraint, even better.

You can enhance a mood of peace or tension by externals like the weather – a storm or spectacular sunset.

Decide which are the big scenes and work towards them and spread them through the book to build up anticipation. These scenes should be significant and change the story or the character. They are likely to be long, so you could have a short, fast scene immediately before for contrast.

Don't stop in the middle of an exciting scene to explain something. You have to get the information in earlier so that the reader understands what's happening and the significance, or explain it later if you can do so without it appearing like something you forgot to put in.

You can start in the middle of a scene, perhaps a quarrel, to increase the pace.

Viewpoint

Viewpoint is what creates atmosphere and makes characters notice different things according to who they are and the moods they are in. There are various types of viewpoints. Where the writer behaves like an all-powerful external agency and is able to see into every character's mind and show his or her thoughts, motivations and intentions, we call it the omniscient viewpoint. It's the condescending 'Dear Reader' syndrome. Today this is considered old-fashioned.

Variations

Novels use either first or third person viewpoints, though some are using a mixture, usually first person narration for the main character and third when in other viewpoints. There is also a trend today of using the present tense rather than the more normal past tense. They are all valid devices but, to begin with, new writers are probably better served using the past tense and third person.

First person

This, (I did, said, thought, etc.) is when the story is told as if by a character. It can cause problems because the reader can see only what that character sees or is told, and it may be difficult to have that character present at crucial times, or finding out important information.

It also risks, with the repetition of 'I', making the narrator sound self-absorbed or boastful. Self-description is difficult, encouraging clichés like the mirror or a friend describing you to your face. If you use first person you must become that character and not be yourself.

Third person

For many writers, especially at first, this is the easiest and commonest viewpoint to use. It overcomes a lot of the technical difficulties of plotting which the first person approach causes. Here the narrator is external, but showing what happens through the eyes of one character at a time.

It can be the same character throughout, and is in most short novels, but it can be done through several viewpoints which change frequently. It's best not to head-hop (change within scenes) as this can confuse the reader who may not follow the narrator into another character's mind. Jumping to another viewpoint for even a moment destroys the bond between the reader and the current viewpoint character. Head-hopping occasionally can work if there's a strong, dramatic reason for change and the reader knows immediately, but swapping viewpoints is more likely to confuse readers instead of having them concentrate on the story. It's best to have a scene break when you change viewpoints. To indicate this leave an extra line or insert an asterisk between the scenes.

Choose the viewpoint character for each scene depending on whose emotions are the most intense or interesting to the reader. Make it consistent and appropriate. Get into that viewpoint by the second sentence of a scene so that the reader knows who it is. Don't tell the reader something the viewpoint character can't know.

Viewpoint patterns

When you have a complex plot you will often have a multi-viewpoint pattern and you need to make smooth transitions from one viewpoint to another. When switching viewpoints make it clear at once, as with flashbacks, that there's a switch. It's very irritating to the reader if the 'he' of the second scene appears to be the same one from the first for several paragraphs. There are many devices you can use.

You can show a transition by a change of time. This can be a straight '*The next day*' or a switch from dusk to midday sun. A change of place can be shown similarly with a change from a scene in a building to '*Back on the farm*' or '*The boat swung broadside as they cast off.*'

You can have a lead-in paragraph, such as a speech by a character who wasn't in the earlier scene. You could have an echo from the first to the next scene, like a repeated word, phrase or action, perhaps by a different character, or you can use simple summary or exposition. For example, Scene 1 ends '*I'll tell David when I see him tonight.*' and the next scene starts with a different character asking '*Did Betty tell you, David?*'

Indicate the pattern of viewpoint switching to the reader at an early stage. If you have several viewpoints, use them early on, not halfway through the book, to get the reader accustomed to it.

Tell only what the viewpoint character can see, hear or experience. They can see another character laugh, frown, cry or shout, and predict his emotion, but they can't see inside his head and know precisely what he is thinking or what actions he is planning.

Keep the reader's interest

This is essential – readers want to get to the end to know what happens to the characters. They want to be drawn from page to page. It's the sign of a good storyteller when this happens, but storytelling is a difficult skill to learn. There are some pointers, apart from an intriguing plot and good characterisation.

Readers will continue

They will want to read on when your characters are interesting, when what they are doing matters, and if their aims are laudable.

Readers will continue if your characters are intriguing, and tempt him to want to know more about them and care what happens to them, or when your plot is exciting, but plausible, and has unexpected twists and turns.

Prolonging the suspense

You entice the reader further by continually posing fresh questions to which he wants the answers, but in giving the answers you pose a further question. Don't explain everything at once. If a girl sees her lover in a compromising situation and he explains how innocent it all was in the next scene, and she believes him, there would be little tension. If the police catch the murderer leaving the scene of the crime covered in blood and carrying the blunt instrument, there is no mystery. If the enemy captures the castle in Chapter One there is no suspense.

Suspense is also created by making promises to your reader, by how the story starts and what expectations you arouse, that the book will be exciting or thrilling. Readers become involved as the characters they like face dangers or suffering. They can be angry at some injustice or perplexed by a mystery. The pressure of a time factor enhances suspense. Mystery helps.

Flashbacks

This is something writers often find difficult to do. These are scenes from the past and are often used from a desire to show and not tell. They can also be used to change a mood or vary the pace. They tend to be overused, however, so avoid them if you can, especially near the end of the book when all should have been explained earlier, or in the middle of a tense scene. They stop the action, interrupt the continuity, can be confusing and prevent the reader from getting on with the story to come, which is usually more interesting to him.

Almost always they slow down the story, wrenching the reader from what is happening, destroying tension which may have been painstakingly built up, or breaking into the reader's expectation, as well as delaying some explanation.

In most cases you can insert the information in some other way. It can be referred to in conversation, revealed gradually through dialogue or brief reflections, or elicited by questions from other characters.

Transitions

Sometimes flashbacks are necessary or the best or only way of conveying information. Take great care with the transitions, both into and out of the previous time. These are difficult and often writers take an easy option which, because it has been used so much by others, is clichéd.

When they are used make certain the reader knows it's a flashback and when it starts and finishes. A frequent method is to have a character remember something, prompted by what happens now, drop into the flashback scene as if experiencing it, then return to the original scene.

The switch can be within the character's thoughts, as he recalls it, but shown in 'real time', as though it's happening now. Or the character could say something like '*That reminds me of the time when -* ', and then the flashback drops into real time instead of having the characters talking about it having happened in the past.

It's often simpler to enter the flashback directly. If you have separate sections within your chapters, divided by a few extra blank lines or an asterisk, you can move straight in. You must indicate as soon as possible, as with any change of scene, that it is a new place, time or viewpoint. Try to do this in the first sentence. Use the past perfect tense only briefly to set the scene and clarify the jump back in time, then revert to the simple past tense, since continuous '*had said*' or '*had thought*' is clumsy. You can return to the main narrative in similar ways, by a scene break or by indicating we are somewhere else.

A flashback will finish either at the end of a scene or chapter, or if it's a short one contained within another scene, by making it perfectly clear we are back in the main story. There are various ways of doing this, by referring to the flashback as something in the past, or switching back to a character present in the main scene but not in the flashback, or by picking up the action or conversation which was interrupted by the flashback.

Flashbacks must be interesting in themselves. The reader wants to get on with what's happening now and will lose interest and patience if he is bored by a lengthy flashback which he doesn't perceive as relevant to the present.

Flashes forward

These are often prologues which are extracts from later in the book, but also can come as hints of future events, foreshadowing. They need to be done very carefully as pointers.

Have, for example, a character planning what to do or looking forward to better times. If, say, a dog is to play an important part later on in the story, mention the dog a couple of times well before the time of the action. If you have a character who is an expert in something, and you need him to use his expertise to help others, mention the fact that he's such an expert some time previously. You could be accused of using coincidence if he is suddenly brought in without warning.

Avoid at all costs the heavy-handed authorial interjection of such predictions as '*she didn't know that next year she would have lost everything.*' This is stepping out of the character's viewpoint and into the omniscient authorial one.

Using appropriate language

As well as trying to convey in a subtle manner the historical feel of the time by the language you use, you will be developing a voice, a style of your own.

Clarity is vital

Say what you mean. It sounds obvious, but if you have any confusion in your own mind about what you want to say it will also confuse readers. You need precision both in words and grammatical construction.

Clarity is best achieved by simplicity. When writers try to produce what they (and unfortunately some English and creative writing tutors) consider 'artistic' prose, their work seems too ornate, over-embellished and often strained as they try to achieve some effect. Simple writing can be as good and beautiful and moving as any other type. If the writer knows exactly what he wants to say, how he wants the reader to understand it, and says it in the clearest and most precise way, it will work for him and the reader.

As well as checking your writing for its meaning, ask whether the sentences are varied, some short, some long. Make sure they are not all the same rhythm and structure and particularly that they are not too long and complicated. Do the same for paragraphs.

Choosing the most effective words

Aim for brevity and lucidity. A strong verb is better than a qualifying adverb. '*He strolled*' is more vivid than '*he walked slowly*'. An exact noun is better than a dozen adjectives. '*Iceberg*' is better than '*a large, floating lump of frozen water*'.

Of course this does not mean you can never use adverbs and adjectives, but use them sparingly, and when you are revising make sure each one is necessary. Watch for the phrases that are so common they have become clichés – like '*bouncing baby*' or '*brakes squealing*'.

Be wary of modifiers again

When an adverb or adjective comes before the verb or noun it is modifying, particularly if there are several intervening words, it is weak, since we don't yet know what it is modifying. Words like rather, quite, a little, also weaken the effect. *'She was rather beautiful'*, and *'he was quite angry'* are not very forceful or interesting comments.

Be positive

Show characters experiencing the external world and use specific examples instead of generalisations. Instead of *'it was very windy'*, you can convey the information more vividly if you have the wind blow a leaf into a character's face. Avoid passive verbs and tenses. *'He watched'* is more forceful than *'he was watching'*. *'He frowned'* is better than *'he looked annoyed'*. *'The dog barked'* is more direct than *'there was a sound of a dog barking'*.

What is style?

It's a whole amalgam of your choice of words, the rhythms of your sentence and paragraph structure, the details you choose to select, your main story focus, and it is evident on your first page. It tells the reader what to expect.

Every writer has certain mannerisms but try to make sure they are not showing too frequently or obtrusively. Try to make sure you are not imitating another writer, which is surprisingly easy to do, particularly if you've just read and enjoyed a book.

Use the appropriate style

We all develop different styles, and we usually write in several different styles depending on our readers and what we are writing. Just as we would make a formal letter of complaint sound very different from telling that complaint to our best friend, the different genres need different approaches.

Some writers write for more than one genre. They adapt their style depending on what they are aiming for – romances, crime stories, science fiction or horror. Within the broad sector of romantic novels, there are styles which are more appropriate for sweet, sexy, saga, historical or suspense stories.

Emotion

Scenes of bustle and excitement require a fast pace, others need time for luxuriating in the detail and the emotions. You will need to show many emotions, but make them clear to the reader. Don't allow unexplained or extreme swings of emotion without a very good cause.

It can be difficult, when describing emotions, to avoid being clichéd or melodramatic. Use images to convey what a character is feeling. In many historicals there will be romantic love scenes which deal with emotion.

Build in tension

For any emotion, try to build up to it, gradually increasing the tension, enjoying it yourself and letting readers do so too.

Questions to answer and things to do

1. If you have ever suffered from writer's block, try to find the cause and make plans to avoid it in future.
2. Make a list of the reasons you've given yourself (or others) for not writing. Were they a hundred per cent truthful?
3. Make a note of different ways you may have tried to overcome writer's block and what works, in what situations.
4. Analyse flashbacks in a published book, see how each is introduced, how long it is and how it is concluded. Was it necessary or could it have been done differently?
5. Analyse a published book and note when characters are introduced and how much is said about them a) then, and b) later.

6. In your book, mark your scene summary for fast, medium and slow-paced scenes. Use different coloured pens so that you can see the pattern. Have you too many of the same pace coming together?
7. Have you used flashbacks only where essential?
8. Could you convey the same information in a different way?

Tips by example

Let's look at the scenes from my second suggested plot and decide which viewpoint to use in each so that they are most effective.

1946		
June	Marion and father	They disagree about her wanting a job

Since Marion is the main character her viewpoint would allow me to show her feelings and gain sympathy from the reader.

June	Marion and Peggy	At school Marion talks about the row, and Peggy says she's lucky to have a father

Peggy's viewpoint would allow her feelings to show, but we may need to show how Marion might feel rather embarrassed after her complaining. This can be done through dialogue and, since Peggy is another major character, it's a good idea to get her viewpoint established early on.

June	Jennifer and Head	Jennifer explaining she has to get a job, cannot stay on at school or go to university

Jennifer's viewpoint to explain her feelings, much the same as with Peggy to establish her character.

June	Peggy	Has telegram at home, afraid, but not about her father

Peggy is alone, so has to be her viewpoint.

July	Marion and mother	Tries to explain feelings to unsympathetic mother

Marion can be showing her thoughts too.

July	Jennifer	She is looking for a job in the town where they live

Jennifer will meet other people, but they are not likely to be important in the story, or not yet, so her viewpoint is best.

Key points

1. You can overcome writer's block.
2. Control the pace and vary it.
3. Be aware of viewpoint and choose appropriately.
4. Keep the readers interested by great characters and an intriguing plot.
5. Use flashbacks very sparingly.
6. Make your language clear, using simple effective words.

10 Research is essential

Most readers like to learn something in a painless way when they read fiction, but they want to absorb information within the story, not have it delivered to them as an academic treatise. Scatter the facts a few at a time where they fit in with the story, but never stop the action while you are giving the reader some information. You have to include some facts in all novels, since too many vague statements make the story unsatisfactory.

The facts you need are like foundations, essential to hold up the structure, but often hidden or noticed only in passing. You will almost certainly research more than you include, but having a greater knowledge of the background facts will enable you to select the essential, relevant ones for the purposes of your story.

The right amount

Don't include anything which is not relevant to the story just because you have found the information or you think it's an interesting snippet. Don't give lectures. It's better to allude to something indirectly than drop out of a character's viewpoint to explain.

Ask whether the information is necessary for the reader's expectations. Historicals will contain more factual details than category contemporary novels.

Does the reader need them to understand the story? Or to believe in the story? Facts provide colour or illuminate the setting.

How much

How much research you need to do depends on how deeply you need to delve into a subject for the purposes of your story. Decide what you need to know, but normally you will get much more information than you will eventually use. This information isn't wasted because it will influence how you look at things and subconsciously colour the way you write about them.

There are different levels of research. First there is the general background, which will become very familiar to you if you write more novels set in the same period or area. Then you will need more specific information, relating more closely to the location and the time, and finally tiny details to illustrate something in the story, to back up some action or make a plot development possible.

If, despite all your efforts, you cannot discover some particular fact, don't fudge and assume something. There's always a chance someone else will know the real fact and there are always methods of getting around it. You can avoid mentioning it or say it in general rather than specific terms, or find a way of doing whatever you need to do in a different way.

Primary sources

These include the landscape, the buildings and artefacts as well as documents. They are objects generated at the actual time, such as clothing, catalogues, journals, diaries, newspapers, photographs, paintings and city directories. You can see many of them in museums and specialist libraries, and they are invaluable for discovering what life was really like.

From the ground up

Let us look at places first. Locations change drastically. If you want to visualise how a town or country looked several centuries or even 50 years ago, it often helps to look at several maps from both before and after the time of interest. The British Library has perhaps the largest collection, but many County Record Offices have their own local collections, as do the Public Record Office and the Royal Geographical Society.

You can see the basic shapes of hills and rivers, things which don't change, and the original road system which tends to remain even if the early roads degenerate into secondary ones. You can trace the coming of railways and new roads, and see how towns which may once have been important have been eclipsed by newer or faster-growing ones. This exercise can itself give you ideas for plots.

To illustrate this, look at several maps of an area you know well and note the differences over time.

In detail

Looking for more detail, let's say of towns and buildings, there are maps that show old fortified cities and the lines of their walls and other defences. If a battle or siege is part of your book these maps are invaluable in showing why the action happened as it did, and looking at them while you read an account of the fight is worth pages of verbal description. It helps you to see not only what happened, but why.

Use maps

Large-scale maps show great detail of houses. In the countryside these will be scattered and they won't all still be there. Field names might be shown, and inns and farms. Town maps tend to be less detailed until the last century or so, but these can still provide important information. The larger-scale Ordnance Survey maps can be very informative.

In *The Glowing Hours*, which was set in the Ladywood and Edgbaston areas of Birmingham, two very different areas within a mile of one another, there were three types of houses I used from the detail on large-scale maps. Various characters lived in each type. There were the back-to-back slums in tiny courts, the larger semi-detached houses with long strips of back garden, and the huge villas with their own extensive grounds. Having selected appropriate homes for some of the characters, I could use details of the routes they took, such as the roads they went along and the pubs they passed and other local landmarks they saw. This gave a sense of place.

Getting the 'feel' of other times and places

You can't visit other times so have to depend on the memories of older people, if it's within their lifespan, or written and other sources. You can visit places, and many writers, though not all, insist on visiting their locations before or during writing about them.

Visit houses and buildings

There are so many of these open to the public you could spend all your time doing this. Be selective, choose those which would have been there at the time of your story, especially if they are furnished in that period or earlier. Remember, as with today, people would have had older furniture, not just what was contemporary to them.

Go to smaller houses where merchants lived, for instance, not only the big stately homes. And don't forget historic gardens, which may not still have a house or may have a much newer house than you want.

There are also many industrial buildings now preserved and open to the public, such as mills and factories, small workshops and shops.

Get organised

You won't remember everything you see or ideas that strike you as you go round, even if there is a guidebook you can buy. Be ready to make notes. You can use a notepad, but if you have a small dictating machine it might be more efficient if you can use this and transcribe notes afterwards. Don't forget to take a camera.

Prepare your questions

Try to read up about the house and prepare before you go. Think what you need to find out and note these things down to remind you when you are there.

If you have written your first draft, having initially researched the location from maps and history and guide books, you will have a better idea of what further details you need to know. You may wish to attend a special event, so you may have to arrange your visit well in advance. If you can choose your time, remember that sightseeing is more comfortable in summer, but museums and libraries might be less busy in winter. Check the times and days of opening.

When you get there

You should already have some idea of the geography, the flora, fauna, climate and landmarks from your preliminary research. You may have seen photographs of typical architecture, both public and private buildings.

What you now need is the ambience of the place. You will get a better idea of this if you use the same modes of transport, the same shops and the same restaurants as the locals do. Talk to as many locals as possible and, if you know of anyone who lives there, try to get an introduction. A neighbour's daughter, for instance, might work there and be willing to meet you. Notice how the locals speak, listen to accents, inflections, rhythms and dialect words.

Keep a diary with your impressions and all the small, normally unimportant details you might need for realism in your plot, such as how long it takes to walk between places. Take photos, of ordinary things as well as tourist sites. Collect every possible souvenir. By this, I don't mean load your baggage with local ashtrays and dolls in national costume, but brochures of hotels and nearby attractions. Many of these are freely available from libraries and information offices and help to supply odd details which you may include in your story.

You could buy local newspapers, books on local history, postcard views, street maps, perhaps a local telephone directory. As well as the obvious physical details, try to decide on the more intangible aspects – the atmosphere, the sounds and smells and any local problems or attitudes which could have influence on people living at the time of your story.

If your location is a foreign one, there will be different weather, food, drink and recreations. A capital or big city will differ from a small town, where there may be greater mutual friendliness amongst the locals who know everyone.

Although you may have a firm idea of the story you want to write, be aware of further dramatic plot possibilities you may perceive from things you discover. When I was researching my book *Masquerade for the King*, I read about the quicksands in St Malo Bay and they gave me an idea for disposing of an enemy. Ask what kind of characters would fit into this setting. Look for new ideas for future books.

Living history museums

These are more popular than ever, and if you need to see how ordinary people lived, people whose houses did not usually survive for long, visit some of these. In England there is the Black Country Museum and Blists Hill, the Victorian town near Ironbridge. In both there are shops and houses, workshops and offices. There are several outdoor museums where old buildings have been reconstructed, such as the Chiltern Museum. In America there are many, but especially impressive are the ones at Williamsburg and Plymoth.

Talking to older people

If your novel is set in the recent past, personal memories of how things were can be invaluable and throw up all sorts of details. Oral history is now recognised for its value and many interviews have been recorded. You may wish to do some of your own. If you are nervous about this you could interview a friend for practice or perhaps an older relative about your own family history.

Doing interviews yourself

Prepare well, and if the person being interviewed allows a tape recorder, put this somewhere unobtrusive and try to forget it and make your interviewee forget it. Have lots of questions ready but be willing to permit the talk to wander in unexpected directions. Your interviewee will be more relaxed and will be able to pull out long-forgotten incidents as other details mentioned remind them of the past. Interpose your next question when there is a pause in the flow of recollections. Don't jump in too quickly, though. If you think there is more to add, a long pause may encourage the interviewee to go on speaking.

Other accounts

These interviews do not have to be on tape. There have been many written accounts such as the books produced by the Women's Institutes in each county, *Within Living Memory*, of their members' reminiscences, and numerous personal memoirs, usually published locally by small presses and sometimes based on interviews, which are wonderful for detail and contemporary attitudes. These are often available in local bookshops, and libraries have the older volumes.

Watching re-enactments

There are scores, if not hundreds, of groups which meet to re-create life in past centuries, have craft displays, exhibitions of old vehicles, weaponry and fighting methods, or re-enact battles and other events. They normally specialise in a particular period, which can be anything from the Stone Age to the present day, and there are even futuristic groups. An address for obtaining a comprehensive list is in the Appendix.

The best re-enactment societies do their utmost to be historically accurate, using contemporary materials and manufacturing methods to make what they need. At their events and fairs and markets you can talk to many people who have become experts in something and who can often answer your questions. And there is nothing like experiencing the sight and sound of a long-ago battle to make you know what it was like to be there. Look for advertisements locally and go to visit an historical re-enactment or exhibition.

Secondary sources

These are usually biographies and histories. Beware of possible inaccuracies and, if you find contradictions, check against another source and take the majority of three versions.

Libraries

Most novels can be researched through the resources of local libraries, visits and maps, but you may need extra local detail.

Your local library ticket can sometimes be used at other libraries, both for reference and borrowing, so check whether this is possible.

Check opening times before you go and whether you need to book time on a machine such as a microfiche reader, or have special documents brought from a distant store. Ask if you need a reader's ticket. If so, how do you get one now instead of wasting time when you get there.

You may need to make a preliminary visit to sort this out, see what's available and consult catalogues, but once there you can talk to the librarians and make arrangements for any special facilities you might need next time you go.

Keeping and organising notes

You can devise your own method of keeping notes – folders, file cards, computer records. Whatever the method, make sure you can locate information easily.

Record where the information was found, the names of people interviewed, when and where. It's surprising how often it's necessary to refer to a source again or verify facts.

Using libraries

The really big ones are the Copyright libraries, which carry an almost complete range of published books and where you are likely to be able to see virtually any book or periodical you need.

These are the British Library and the University libraries at Oxford, Cambridge, Edinburgh, Aberystwyth and Dublin.

If you go to one of the major libraries be aware that they are huge buildings and may be scattered on several sites. It may take hours or even days to bring your requested material from distant stacks. If they run induction sessions, try to attend, especially if you plan to use that library frequently. Otherwise you'll waste a lot of time just finding your way round.

The larger city reference libraries are in Belfast, Birmingham, Cardiff, Edinburgh, Glasgow, Liverpool, London (Westminster) and Manchester. These might be easier for you to get to and quite possibly might provide all you need.

The British Library, for which a reader's ticket is needed and for some departments a letter of recommendation, is perhaps the most comprehensive collection of documents, maps and books, with music, sound and newspaper collections too. There are many ancient documents, Oriental and India Office collections and they have Science and Social Policy Information services too. Most of the collections apart from the Newspaper Library are now located at the new building in St Pancras.

The specialists

For many other specialist libraries you will need a ticket and perhaps a reference, you may have to prove your need for the research or that the books or sources are not available elsewhere. Fees may be charged on a daily or hourly basis so enquire first.

Many museums and art galleries have libraries. There are large ones such as the National Maritime Museum, the Natural History Museum and the Royal Botanical Gardens. Cathedrals and government organisations have libraries, as do many private organisations such as businesses.

There are many local history centres and county record offices attached to the main lending and reference libraries. There are libraries for costume, folklore, medicine, religion, science, the theatre, toys, transport and many more. Ministries, Embassies, or professional organisations may all be able to help with specific queries.

For most of these libraries research will take time. Some are open for relatively short periods or can only answer specific queries by post. Librarians are paid to direct you to the appropriate resources, not to do the work for you, but they will often be of great help. They might be able to assemble the best material before you arrive if you tell them what you need in advance.

It's useful to have an address file for specialist libraries and other organisations you may need to consult because of your particular interests and needs.

Useful material

As well as books on particular times or topics, if you want to get a background of a particular place, look at the local directories such as Kelly's, which give a brief description and history of the town or village, details of the main buildings and lists of gentlemen, farmers and tradesmen in the area.

You can discover, for instance, how many public houses or drapers' shops there were, their names and locations, and you can also, to avoid potential problems, ensure that the names you have selected for your imaginary characters do not inadvertently repeat the name of a real person or a real business.

In *The Cobweb Cage*, I needed a chemist's shop where rather dubious activities happened so I had to make sure the name I used was not one that existed.

But you can mention, in passing, that your character visited a certain hostelry or bought her bread from a certain baker. My character bought material from a shop that really existed. Other real people such as the School Attendance Officer and the Matron of a local hospital were mentioned. I found all this information in a Kelly's Directory. That doesn't compromise the real people, but adds verisimilitude.

Finding information in libraries and museums

There are guides to museums and special collections, World Guides to Libraries, Special Libraries, Western Europe and Central & Eastern Europe.

Many library catalogues are now on CD-ROMs, online computers or microfiche.

Exploring archives

There are national and local archives which could be of use to you.

The Public Record Office

A great many state documents are kept at the Public Record Office in Kew. Tel 020 8876 3444 for information about tickets. Other important historical collections are in the London Guildhall Library, The Foreign and Commonwealth Office Library, and the Imperial War Museum.

Local archives

Make friends with the archivist. Most county libraries have huge stocks of material and it's not always easy, even when familiar with the catalogues, to find what you need. Archivists are usually anxious to help and to direct you towards possible sources.

As well as books on the area and local people, and registers from churches and local government, such as marriages and voters' lists, they have collections of photographs, and documents such as letters, bills and receipts. You may need to consult the local judiciary proceedings and census records, which can often supply information on the population, types of occupations and density of housing.

Museums

There are many of these, often devoted to one particular thing like costume, dolls' houses or the leather industry. Some are open infrequently so check before you go.

Art galleries

These are useful for studying landscape, interiors, and portraits of the time, and their bookshops often have useful volumes on specific topics.

Photographs

There are books published in every small town containing collections of photographs of the localities showing what the towns used to look like. These are invaluable if, as has so often happened, the centre of the town has been ripped out to build a shopping centre or the High Street has been changed by new shop fronts. One of the reasons I set *The Cobweb Cage* in the small town of Hednesford was because the High Street had not been greatly changed.

Films, videos and music

Old films on TV, and historical drama and documentaries on both TV and radio, can provide valuable information. Try to video or record anything useful and then make notes to add to your records. There are lots of videos, CDs or DVDs available of old films, recent TV adaptations, scenic journeys and much more.

Videos and audio tapes are available commercially and through libraries for a small charge. Ask what's available. The producers strive for historical accuracy, and apart from specific information you may glean, you can acquire an impression of life at a particular time. However, watch out for inaccuracies on films and videos. Their research is not necessarily perfect. Double check everything.

Try to listen to tapes of music played on old instruments, and if possible go to performances where you may be able to talk to the players and even examine the instruments. Hearing something played as it was originally intended, on the instruments of the day, can give a totally different impression to modern renditions. Music on contemporary instruments sounds quite different to when it is being played on modern versions. There are CDs and DVDs of these too.

Newspapers and magazines

Look for advertisements, prices, local colour, jobs and wages offered. Combing through newspapers can take a great deal of time, but if you narrow down your search to a specific period you will find fascinating snippets, and not only in the obvious columns.

As well as the news reports, read the letters pages, the editorials, obituaries, and, if relevant, the proceedings of the local councils and societies. You often get different viewpoints which might stimulate your imagination and give you ideas for areas of conflict.

For price comparisons, read the job advertisements, the 'For sale' columns and the display advertisements from local businesses. They often show clothing, with the prices, and this gives you an idea of how much a character might spend on certain purchases. You can obtain photocopies from the microfilm readers of anything especially valuable to you, and where there is a great deal of detail and it would be tedious to make comprehensive notes, this can be useful for future checking.

Use the internet

Use it if possible because a good deal of the official archive material you may need is on it, but be aware of inaccuracies.

What is the internet?

This is an incredibly valuable tool for any researcher. Apart from research, you can send e-mail messages instantly to the far side of the world at a fraction of the cost of fax, phone or 'snail mail'.

It is obviously more convenient if you have Internet access yourself and can explore the facilities at any time, but this can be expensive. There are cyber cafés in most large towns and some libraries provide terminals, available for an hourly fee, where you can try it out, or for occasional use.

Competition is bringing down the cost, but most people find they spend far more time connected than they imagine.

What's available

You can access libraries, universities, museums, art galleries, newspapers and magazines, buy books or houses, look at travel and book flights or holidays, and you can post questions to relevant Newsgroups, where someone is likely to be able to help you.

Many writers have set up their own Web page. If you access mine at www.marina-oliver.net you will find lists of my books, a few extracts and other information. You can join chat groups or e-mail loops and chat to other writers, read reviews and contact writers' groups. The danger is the distraction you may find.

Even if you hate technology, just look at a demonstration of the Internet, at a cyber café, with a friend who's 'online' or in a large computer store.

Balancing research and imagination

This is the skill of a successful historical novelist. Below is a brief summary of how I combined real and imaginary facts in *Runaway Hill*.

An example of weaving in real events to the plot

The real events are in italics, and my fictional story was plotted to take advantage of them, the locations, and the brief appearances of real historical characters.

1642   Heroine Drusilla is sent from her home, Devizes, where she has refused to marry an older, wealthy merchant, to stay with her brother James and his family in Reading. She resents the attentions of a stolid young merchant, Jacob Blagrave, who tells them about *the battle of Edge Hill, that October.*

The King begins to advance on London and meets a Parliamentary deputation at Reading. Drusilla meets the hero, the Royalist Sir Randal Thornton, but her brother accepts Jacob's offer for her. She hears of *army looting near Brentford.* James resents *the taxes on merchants for housing the Royalists when they return to Reading, and preparations for a siege.* He leaves to join the Parliamentary army. Drusilla meets Sir Randal again when he comes *with Prince Rupert in December for a mayoral banquet.*

In April 1643 the siege by the Parliamentarians begins, and some daring Royalists attempt to bring reinforcements on river barges. Drusilla again meets Sir Randal who has come with the barges. *The town surrenders and the Royalists leave.* Drusilla refuses to go and stays to protect James's property.

The Parliamentarians begin plundering. Sir Randal comes back, they secretly escape and he takes Drusilla to Devizes. When he asks to marry her she believes it is because they had to stay together at public inns, and he does not mean it, so she refuses and he leaves.

A small Royalist garrison begins to fortify Devizes against attack from Waller's troops ensconced on Roundway Down overlooking the town. The Royalists send relief from Oxford and win the battle. Drusilla's brother is injured and she goes to help him but on the way is attacked and rescued by Sir Randal.

The locals, seeing the Parliamentary army escaping down a steep escarpment, give the battle the name of RUNAWAY HILL, thus giving me my title.

Facts

If you are portraying real people you have to be very careful to maintain accuracy. You can discover facts, or many of them, through research. What you can't discover you have to imagine. But keep any invented actions to what is probable, what could have happened.

With imaginary characters it's much easier, but they still need to be recognisable as people within a certain framework of the time and conventions, doing what would have been possible.

Emotions

These are universal, we know about love, hate, jealousy and compassion. Opinions may be influenced by the contemporary mores, but we can empathise with feelings of frustration or joy, whatever the cause.

It isn't easy to know how real characters felt. Even if there are letters and diaries relating what they said they felt, these may not reveal the true inner emotions. We all put on a gloss, a pretence, for public consumption. Only secret diaries never meant for public reading can get near to the truth, although even then the writers may be tempted to portray their own actions as right, or justifiable, or misunderstood by others.

You have to judge what was likely, and the more you immerse yourself in the period and get to know the contemporary world, the social and other constraints, the political situation, whatever is relevant and important to your characters, whether real persons or from your own imagination, the better you will be able to get inside them and show them to the reader.

Avoid showing the research. So slip it in unobtrusively and make it integral.

Sex – sweet or sizzling? sensuous or sexy?

Decades ago authors did not look behind the bedroom door, but as our society became more open about sexual matters, so did authors in how they portrayed sex. Some publishers don't want explicit sex in novels, others do. This is one aspect you have to think about if you aim to write for a specific publisher.

What's acceptable?

Your sex scenes can be anywhere in the range from slight suggestion to overtly clinical. Where you place them depends on your own preferences, but only write what you are comfortable with. If you force yourself to write raunchier detail than you really like it will show.

My own preference is to avoid the clinical 'sex by numbers', as there are relatively few ways of describing sexual acts and repetition becomes boring. Suggestions, leaving the details to the reader's imagination, can be much more effective than too precise details. Concentrate more on the emotions characters feel. And don't forget dialogue. Mix it with the narrative to show what characters are feeling. Bring in the externals, such as the soft scented sheets in a firelit room, or the prickly hay in a cold, dusty loft.

Use your characters

These scenes involve your characters, and you need to consider how they would approach sexual encounters, from the slightest touch to full intercourse, inside marriage or not. Don't forget, either, how they might feel afterwards.

Outside marriage

The possibility of extra-marital sex will depend on a variety of things. Do they live in a permissive age and place, such as the Restoration Court, or a very secretive society such as the Victorian middle class? Or a repressive Puritan one as in seventeenth century New England? Are they influenced by the teachings of their religion? What constraints, physical and moral, are there? If they want secrecy, how likely are they to be found out? What opportunities do they have? I'm sure everyone can make opportunities if they try hard enough, so this could be part of your plot.

Were girls closely guarded or free to follow their own desires? This will depend on time and class. There would normally be the fear of pregnancy, so how much of a deterrent would this be? Would an illegitimate child be accepted or a disaster? Would it be absorbed into the mother's family, or would she be forced to hide and bear her 'shame' in secret?

In Victorian times especially, respectability was very important. Social attitudes, the fear of being cast out by family or friends, can be vital in certain times and places.

People in all times and from all sorts of families would have extra-marital affairs, though, face the risks and flout convention. What forces are strong enough to make them do so?

Rape

Not many authors allow their heroes to be rapists. Readers are unlikely to sympathise. The victim, however, has to deal with the consequences, the anger, fear, possibly self-blame. How badly it affects her can depend on how sheltered a life she led previously.

Treat rape scenes graphically if it fits with your plot, or show as little of the violence and horror as you feel necessary. I am, too, always astonished at the high proportion of fictional rapes that result in pregnancy. It has become a cliché in some sorts of historicals.

In the marriage bed

Within marriage attitudes to sex varied. You need to consider their social class. Is it a time when women were supposed not to enjoy sex? This is the 'Lie back and think of England' attitude. Some girls might know little of what sex entailed, and we hear of many who were shocked and disgusted on their wedding nights.

How do your characters fit into these roles? How much will they know? Have they lived in the country and seen animals mating? Have they friends who might have imparted knowledge – or incorrect information? Have they lived in one room where privacy was impossible?

It could be the fault of inept husbands. Is he tender and caring, or concerned only with his own satisfaction? Has he had experiences with prostitutes or, in many cases, married lovers? You need to know the past history of your characters, and how this will have affected or moulded them in order to give them convincing sex scenes.

Useful reference books

As you write more you will build a library of the books used most frequently. Some are general, but you will have special interests depending on the type of novel you write, such as historical or crime. If you use a multi-media computer, CDs and DVDs are available, and soon we'll all be using the Internet, but books may still be preferred by many people.

Books to look for

1. A good encyclopaedia and a dictionary, as big as you can afford, are investments. You will be consulting them far more frequently than you imagine.
2. One of the yearbooks for writers, the *Writers' and Artists' Yearbook* or *The Writer's Handbook*, even an out of date

one, will be of value as both give lengthy lists of agents and publishers.

3. Spelling dictionaries are quicker to use than an ordinary one.

4. A thesaurus or book of synonyms will help you to avoid repeating words.

5. A dictionary of names will give you ideas, saving you from calling all your minor characters John and Mary Jones. Telephone directories can supply surnames, especially for foreign characters.

6. A book of quotations can provide ideas and titles.

7. Books on grammar, punctuation and style are useful for checking anything you may be unsure of, and most of us have gaps in our knowledge or queries on language and usage.

8. Books by writers about their own experiences and discoveries are good for tips on techniques and can be fascinating.

9. There are many specialist guides and 'How To' books to help with particular types of writing. They vary from the succinct to the discursive, so check several before you buy to make sure you get one you will find of practical value.

10. Maps, guidebooks and pamphlets, as well as hotel directories, will provide many local details.

11. There are numerous small books on a huge variety of subjects, like the Shire books, detailed enough to tell you the basics without being too technical and overwhelming.

12. Don't ignore books for children, either. They can be excellent in revealing the real core of a subject.

Questions to answer and things to do

1. Look in a large bookshop and make a list of the reference books you would like to acquire. Could these go on a birthday present list?

2. Make lists of local libraries, museums, historic houses and other places you may find useful to visit. Note the opening hours and telephone numbers.

Tips by example

For my second suggested novel set in the 1950s, I would need to find out about the training of nurses, the situation regarding soldiers lost during the war, wages and prices, as well as the general background of houses, costume and other domestic matters. I would be able to talk to people who lived then and might be able to visit houses which have not been changed much. I would need maps of the time, since a lot of building has been done since then. This would be just the start of my research, but local archives would have a wealth of useful material.

Key points

1. Only a small percentage of what you research will go into the novel.
2. Use maps, especially large-scale ones.
3. Visit locations.
4. Prepare before you go.
5. Make notes while you are there.
6. Use libraries, in particular specialist ones, and archives.
7. Explore the Internet.

11 **Revision**

You've reached the end of your novel. Well done! You thought you had almost finished? I'm sorry, but there is still a great deal to do.

Some writers hate the chore of revising. Other would-be writers never seem to finish anything, but may have drawers full of notes. Some enjoy revising more than creating the original draft.

Editing your work

First drafts, revision and polishing are all essential if you are to be successful. What is most important to you? Is it getting something down quickly, starting new projects, polishing and revising your work or finishing it? If you rarely finish, have you asked yourself why?

Don't waste your efforts

Complete the first draft quickly, however roughly. Don't try to do too much detailed revision until you have this completed, in that it has reached the end of the story. There is the danger of spending so much time on the opening that you never get to the end.

Don't spend too much time as you go

It's a great temptation to keep going back over what you've done. You can always find things to change. Even when a script has been completed, writers tinker. They are perhaps reluctant to let it go out into a hard, hostile world.

Try not to go back too much while doing the first draft, unless you get to a complete dead end and have to alter something vital for the plot to work. It's better to finish your first draft, prove you can write a whole novel, then start revising. Some experienced writers revise as they go, but many do a very fast first draft and spend far longer on the revising stage. It is useful, especially for beginners, to have something, however faulty, to work on. It still needs more. And professionals don't usually send out work until it has been thoroughly revised.

You have completed a whole book. Correction – you have written a first draft, perhaps making some alterations along the way, doing some revision. You are probably eager to send your novel to a publisher, but wait. Don't be in too much hurry. Is it good enough yet? First thoughts are not necessarily the best and revising can make the difference between failure and acceptance. Everything you write can be made better and time spent on revision makes all the difference, as professionals know. The experienced writer knows that revision, whenever done, is the most important, often most difficult task. Most writers I know do three or more drafts.

Take a break

Before this revision, put the typescript away for as long as you can. After a break, you will come back refreshed and faults are easier to spot. You can have a blitz on the garden or housework, or go out and see all the friends you've been neglecting.

Keep on writing though. It's fatally easy to get out of the habit. You can write something else, short stories or non-fiction. Distance yourself from your novel, try to forget it, so that when you come back you can judge it objectively. Try to read as if you are new to the story.

Don't be in too big a hurry

Make the break as long as you can reasonably afford to wait, then reread the novel so that it is fresh to you.

Now for the really hard work

Start with a swift read-through, making notes as you go. Revision can be done at several levels, and it's very like the editing and copy editing before a book is published. Then you may prefer to take each element separately, do the revision in stages rather than try to remember all the points you need to consider all at once.

Make it perfect

When you find something wrong or less than perfect, correct it even if it means considerable rewriting.

If there is a fact you cannot check but which a reader could know, leave it out and find another way of saying what it is you need. Don't ever guess if there's a chance you could be proved wrong.

You can start with the details, which is what a copy editor does, or the overall view, the editor's task.

After making alterations, recopy, type, put onto the word processor or reprint it, since this process seems to make work develop even further. Just seeing what you have written in a different format helps you to spot errors and problems.

Rewriting

Rewriting does not mean sitting down and doing the same work again, but differently. This would not be very constructive. It would be the same as another first draft. The same errors would probably creep in while some of the spontaneity, the original first flush of enthusiasm, would be lost.

To begin with, rewriting means going over the piece of work to check for errors, deciding whether certain things might be expressed more clearly and putting points in a different order.

Spotting errors

Do you spot errors in your own work? It is notoriously difficult to see your own mistakes. You are far too close to them and see what you expect to see, what you think you have written. This applies to simple spelling or typing errors and bigger faults, perhaps something that invalidates a whole plot.

Many people find it more difficult to spot errors on a computer screen than on paper. This may change as we become more familiar with using screens, but if you do use a computer it often helps to print out your work and do revisions on paper.

You can also do spell checks on most word processing programs, which will stop silly mistakes reaching the publisher.

But be wary. These will not notice errors of meaning such as effect instead of affect, or practise instead of practice, since all are valid words.

Are you reluctant to change what you have written? You need to overcome this reluctance, because even when a novel has been accepted for publication editors may want quite a lot of changes.

What to look for

When you are rewriting you are effectively editing your work. Your first read-through for revision may be for choosing better words, more precise phrases, correcting typos and punctuation. Editing and sub-editing can mean simply checking for typing errors but ought to be far more.

Check spellings, in particular consistency. Then check grammar, and that the meaning is always clear. If you overuse the same word or expression try to find synonyms. Cut superfluous words and sentences. Cut out everything that isn't essential. Make sure paragraphing is appropriate.

Change words which have been repeated too close together, or too often. Remove superfluous adverbs and adjectives and, if you can, replace these phrases with more appropriate or effective verbs and nouns. Check for clichés, trite expressions or convoluted metaphors.

As you are doing this you may want to change the order of words or passages, rewrite sentences or shift scenes around.

You might need to add or remove a scene. Add if you need to for explanation, remove because the scene doesn't add anything and is just padding.

You may decide to add or remove a character, strand or subplot. It could be better to change a scene to dialogue instead of narrative, write a scene in a different way, put scenes in a different order or rewrite a section from another character's viewpoint or at a different place or time. Have you made it clear when you change viewpoint and have flashbacks?

Check that the point of view is consistent and appropriate, that the length and/or strength of the story can support more than one. If it changes, are the changes signalled early enough for the reader? Are you describing too much?

Watch your language

When you are writing a first draft of your novel, you may not wish to have to pause to find appropriate words for your characters to use when they are speaking, especially if you are trying to give the flavour of the time. At first it will not come very naturally to you, but as you soak yourself in the period it will become easier.

You must be certain to revise. Take the revision of language in two stages.

To begin with, go through your typescript and just look at the speeches. Is the dialogue natural, interesting, necessary and informative? If not you may have to cut it out. Is the language appropriate? Is it vivid and arresting?

Ask whether the language fits the time, whether any words are too modern or out of place? Could any words be changed for better, more appropriate ones? Then read aloud and see whether the speeches sound smooth and easy to say.

Go through again and look at the narrative. Is there too much exposition? Are there too many flashbacks? Have you used any modern slang or anachronistic words? What about imagery? Is it appropriate both to the time and to the situation of your characters? Does it not only fit in with the period, does it do something else?

When you have done this your novel will be taking on an historical aura, some of that essential detail which, while unobtrusive, will take the readers into the period and make them feel and hear and smell the same things as your characters do.

Make sure characters are consistent

This means in appearance, speech, voice, attitudes and behaviour. Ensure your characters do not change name or appearance midway. Make them speak appropriately, using dialect or special speech patterns consistently. Make their behaviour consistent with their characters or motivations. Is every character essential? Make a list of all your minor characters and decide why you have introduced them. Could any of their functions be served by another character so that you could cut down the total number? Do they all have different roles? Could two minor characters be merged?

Are the characters real, convincing? Are they in conflict? Do they develop and grow? Is their behaviour in line with their motivations? Ask if the story pulls the readers along, will they care about the characters and understand everything going on.

Check the plot

Is the story appropriate for the genre? Is the storyline clear? Have you treated your story in an original way? Does the beginning establish setting, viewpoint and mood? Have you started in the right place or too soon in the story? Does the plot move actively towards the conclusion? Did you provide foreshadowing and follow it up?

Write a summary, scene by scene, of your novel. There will probably be several scenes in each chapter, both short and long. For each decide what purpose it serves and, if you cannot be sure that it advances the plot, cut it out.

Look at each scene for its purpose. Are they all complete? Are some scenes too slow or boring? Does each one move the story forward, demonstrate facets of character or tell the reader something relevant and new? If not, why is it there?

Does the action come in the wrong place? Do any important events take place offstage, does the timescale work, is the chronology clear, are there too many flashbacks, are they made clear? Is the tone consistent, is the story complete, have important scenes been skimped, is the pace right, at the start, within, and at the end? Are the chapter breaks in the right places, do they have good end hooks, is the book boring, are some parts too long?

Is anything missing, such as explanations or clues? Are your big scenes in the right places? Does the story flow, so that the events are easily understood by the reader? Is the conflict strong, believable and compelling? Is it resolved satisfactorily? Are all the loose ends tied up?

Look at the structure and ask whether something is at stake. Does the tension build satisfactorily and is the problem resolved convincingly?

Is the resolution satisfactory, arising inevitably out of the story? Are all the sub-plots necessary? Check all the details, make sure you have been consistent and that the timescale is correct. Is the pacing clear? Does the pace vary enough? Have you exploited every situation and emotion fully?

Is description accurate?

This applies to people, places and events. Is there enough detail or too much? Is it specific enough and do the details selected enhance your meaning? Use description accurately, especially of places. Check that daffodils are not blooming in autumn, that journeys can be completed in the time allowed. Make sure you do not have ten days in a week. If you are being very specific as to time or place check factual aspects such as train timetables or routes, weather conditions and pub opening times. Have you weeded out unimportant details?

Look at the imagery. It may be to illuminate the concept or the action, or explain something. Try to make sure you have a purpose for it and have not simply inserted it for no good reason.

In both narrative and dialogue, look out for mentions of sensory ideas. Check them, the sounds and smells, for accuracy.

Question everything

Especially question details you 'know'. As well as the ordinary checking of the manuscript, the revision for consistency, plot credibility, pace and tension and the dozens of other variables, historical novelists need to check their historical facts.

It's best to do this while you are writing the book, so that major problems do not occur later on because you discover a crucial action was, for some reason, impossible. It's also one of the things to be aware of when rewriting, and on final revision. All too often in the flush of original composition we think we know something, can't stop then to check, and forget to make sure afterwards. Much later it may occur to us that we didn't make absolutely sure that bridge was built when we took our characters across it, or they were driving in a carriage which wasn't designed until three years later.

Make notes of any queries, and cross them out when you have found the answers.

Have a final read through

When you are satisfied with every aspect and have a clean, corrected copy using the accepted layout as described in the next chapter, you are almost ready to submit your work. Once more put the novel aside for a while, then reread it so that it is fresh to you. Do something else to fill your mind and get a distant, new perspective.

Can you judge your own work?

It is difficult to judge our own work and you may need impartial advice. Don't rely too much on family, friends or even on writing groups. If you want to sell, there is not much point in asking for sales advice from people who don't know the current market situation. If you belong to a writers' group ask whether their criticism is informed and constructive.

Pay special attention if several people have the same criticism and you think they may have a point. But don't change just because one person says so – people, even editors, don't always agree, and you don't want to spend time changing something only for the next person to suggest you change it back.

You may need help

Do you think you need any specialised help with anything, for example with spelling or punctuation? If so, do you know where to find it? Don't be afraid to ask – people like spouses and friends might be glad to help with these mechanical aspects.

Where can you turn for advice on the marketability of your novel, or get a critical appraisal on the aspects we have been looking at, characterisation, plotting, dialogue, pace and the rest?

You could ask for professional criticism. There are specialist agencies who advertise in writing magazines. In many areas there are Arts Council schemes where you can ask for a professional appraisal. You might find tutors at courses and conferences who will read your work as part of a course.

When you get to the end, stop

Too much tinkering can damage freshness. If you are satisfied it is the best you can do, don't be afraid to send it out. You have to test the reaction. Are you satisfied with your novel, and ready to send it out? Then do!

Questions to ask and things to do

1. Do you get bored with your novel once you have the first draft written? Revision is essential, it's something you need to do if you want to be published.
2. As you reread your novel try to concentrate on one aspect at a time, such as does the plot work, are characters consistent and are the protagonists sympathetic?
3. Check especially for historical inaccuracies or dialogue which is too modern.

Tips by example

Look at my opening paragraphs for the Pepys novel. Let's assume it began differently in the first draft and I will explain why the changes were made.

It was late, a dark winter night, and the naval office had been frantically busy all day, and nothing seemed to have been done. Samuel Pepys, twenty-seven years old, pulled out the notebook in which he recorded his thoughts in the special shorthand he had devised, so that no one else, especially his wife Elizabeth, daughter of the French Huguenot St Michel, to whom he had been married for five years, and who was twenty years old, could read it. It contained too many indiscretions.

This is far too detailed, impersonal, lacks emotion and historical detail, and there is no clear viewpoint character. It contains unnecessary information that could be added later. Change to:

Samuel Pepys threw down the quill, scattered sand over the manuscript, and stretched his aching fingers. Another day's events recorded. It was hard to keep up this diary, after a busy day at the naval office, but it gave him considerable satisfaction and relieved his frustrations to put down his real thoughts, in the knowledge that no one else could pry into his secret language.

'Samuel?' It was his wife Elizabeth calling, and he smiled and stood up.

Especially he didn't want Elizabeth to read his thoughts about their maidservants. A man had to have his little pleasures. He smiled again. Bedtime, and Elizabeth was still young and eager.

This has action, contemporary detail and all the necessary information so that readers can know what is happening. It's in the main character's viewpoint and shows his thoughts.

Key points

1. Get a complete draft of the novel written.
2. Take a break and then return to it to do your revision.
3. Check for the simple errors first.
4. Then look at things such as characterisation.
5. Check for historical accuracy.
6. If you need advice or an appraisal, consult a professional agency.

12 Presentation and publication

It is important to make your typescript as professional as possible.

First impressions

A good first impression is vital, since editors and agents have no time to spend on amateur productions. So we need to help them as much as possible by making their jobs easy. Ideally the parcel should be fast to open, the pages easy to read and the enclosures as little time-consuming as possible. However, always check first that the agent or editor to whom you send the manuscript is willing to consider it, and if they say they want the first three chapters, or fifty pages, send only that, not the entire script.

Layout

Choose a clear typeface, not a fancy one, with a reasonably large font size which will give you about ten to twelve words per line, double spaced on one side only of A4 paper that is thick enough not to allow the page beneath to show through. You need wide margins, especially to the left side of the page, about 3–4 cm. If you use a word processor try to use a laser or inkjet printer, at least for the final copy. Many editors now refuse to read faint dot-matrix type.

Indent all paragraphs about five spaces and don't, as with business correspondence, leave extra space between paragraphs. This looks ugly in dialogue and completely confuses the word count.

Number the pages consecutively, and use an identifying header of your name or title.

Enclosures

With the typescript enclose a brief letter of explanation, a title page with certain details and a synopsis.

Letter

This query letter is the first sample of your writing an agent or editor sees, so it must attract the reader by the style, clarity and the degree of interest it arouses. Provide all essential information about the typescript, for instance the genre, the time and place in which it is set, the characters, theme and some idea of the story. Say something about yourself and any previous writing successes. If you have any special, relevant expertise – mention it.

The letter must be no more than one page, single-spaced, and give an impression of both efficiency and talent. Don't try to draw attention with gimmicks. They will work against rather than for you.

Title page

Have on this your name and address, pseudonym if used, daytime and evening telephone numbers, and fax number or e-mail address if you have them. Also provide an approximate word count. For most publishers a computer count is enough.

Synopsis

This should be no more than three or four pages, double spaced. The objective is to make the agent or editor want to read the whole manuscript. Make it a present tense, continuous narrative, and provide a strong opening hook. Establish the time and place.

Briefly summarise the plot, including the resolution. Agents can judge your style and will meet the characters in the opening pages, but that does not tell them what happens.

Introduce the main characters and explain their conflicts and motivations. Show the pivotal and crisis scenes, and keep it moving and page-turning, as your book is. Mention the theme, and explain the main sub-plots, how the goals are achieved and how characters change. Write in the same style as the script while showing you have done your research.

Write your synopsis, set it aside and reconsider it in a few days.

Approaching an agent or publisher

It is becoming more normal that publishers of mainstream novels read only agented manuscripts, knowing that they have been vetted once and anything completely unsuitable has already been returned. This means you should first look for an agent to take you on as a client.

However, it depends on the publisher and the type of books. There is no particular advantage in having an agent when the contract is a standard one, such as for My Weekly Story Collection (D. C. Thomson) or Harlequin Mills and Boon. Both these publishers will send you guidelines, but the only satisfactory way of knowing what they want is to read lots of their books. MWSC do both historical and contemporary novellas of 30,000 words and HM&B have a historical line, around 85,000 words, where many of the books are Regencies.

Going about it

Look first in one of the yearbooks and do what is asked there. If agents say they have no room for new clients, there is no point in approaching them. If they specify a letter, send just that and always send return postage and a self-addressed envelope or label. If they ask for the first three chapters and a synopsis, send that.

Write rather than phone. Some agents will answer queries by e-mail, but most insist on the typescript being sent on paper, not electronically. This is because they read submissions on the move, in taxis or on their way home, and also they cannot afford to print out the hundreds of submissions they receive.

Try to select appropriate agents. Again the yearbook entries may say which writers agents represent, or what they specialise in. You can discover more personal suggestions by talking to published writers, and try to meet agents at talks, courses or workshops.

It is acceptable to send to several agents at once, unless they say in their yearbook entries that they will not look at multiple submissions. Don't make it a circular letter though. Find out the name of one person in the agency and address it to them. Make sure you tell all the others when one agent agrees to accept you as a client, so that they don't waste their time.

Start by making a list of ten agents who might be interested in your book and send query letters to five. Keep the other five in reserve for the next attempt.

Make life easy for editors

The objective of a writer seeking publication is to give a favourable first impression. One way is to make life easy for the editor considering the script. Very faint lettering, a fancy typeface or letters too small for easy reading will condemn your script, probably unread.

Editors read a lot and need to protect their eyes.

Don't stifle it

Put the script into a simple envelope folder or hold the pages together with a rubber band and post in a strong, padded envelope.

Never pin or staple sheets together or fix them into ringbinders or tie with convoluted nets of string and sailors' knots. Editors don't appreciate being stabbed or having to struggle to open or read a script.

Rejections

An incredibly small proportion of writers can boast they never had a rejection. They are fortunate ones who discovered what they wanted to write at once, were good at it, writing when it was in demand, sent it to the right editor at the right time and have maintained this success.

Even established and successful writers receive rejections.

It doesn't mean your work is bad

A rejection is not a personal insult. It does not mean the work is bad or not worth publishing. There are many reasons an editor cannot use material. You may have sent it to the wrong publisher, or just after they have accepted something very similar, or have too much in hand to take anything else.

Editors are human, have off days and personal preferences, so your work may simply land on their desk when they are not receptive, or may not appeal to them. Much of this is luck.

There are precautions you can take to make as certain as you can your work goes to the right editor, but at the start it is largely good fortune, given the ability to write well, if your work is accepted.

Once you have had an acceptance, take advantage of it. Cultivate that editor and send more work.

Persevering

It is not easy to find either an agent or a publisher, but if your work is good enough and you don't give up, you will eventually succeed. For my 'How To' book, *Writing and Selling a Novel*, I sent questionnaires to many published novelists. Most had spent years and written several books before one was accepted. So don't give up too soon.

Contracts

A contract can be very brief or a long document, and you need an expert to make sure there are no unacceptable clauses. Even though your agent will advise you, read contracts thoroughly and query anything you don't understand or don't like. Terms can often be negotiated and an agent is in a better position than you are to do this on your behalf. The Society of Authors gives advice to members, and once you have been offered a contract they will advise on it before you become a member.

Longer contracts specify who owns second rights, which for novels usually means paperback, large print, audio, book club, foreign and translation editions. Film and TV rights are infrequent, but usually included. Contracts set out what proportions of future sales go to publisher and author, publication timing, whether the author can influence the jacket, number of free copies, disclaimers about unforeseen events which prevent publication, libel, copyright and when the book will be remaindered. Electronic rights also need to be included.

Copyright

Despite recent 'tidying' legislation in the UK, the law of copyright is extremely complicated. It varies in different countries and there is a mass of case law which makes trying to interpret the fine details a specialist task. Because of this, infringements of copyright and subsequent court battles can be very expensive.

To give the simplest possible explanation, copyright applies to an author's rights in his work, which exist as soon as he has written it, before publication. This means that other people cannot quote from a piece of work without the author's permission. It applies to lines of songs or extracts from broadcast scripts. There are exceptions, such as quoting short extracts for purposes of illustration, comment or study, but it would be wise to consult a lawyer before publishing anything you haven't permission to quote. There is no copyright in ideas or titles.

In the UK since January 1996 copyright extends for seventy years after an author's death. A new edition can create a new copyright, so just because an author died over seventy years ago it does not necessarily mean their work is out of copyright and can be quoted freely.

You can give away copyright, and some publishers may ask for this, but it is not a good idea to agree.

Other legal matters

If something is defamatory and published in a permanent form, such as in writing, it may constitute libel. An action for damages can be brought. If you take a living person as a model for your villain and give him derogatory sayings or actions, you could be in trouble. It's wise to check there isn't a clergyman or accountant with the same name in the town where you set your story, or anyone who might, by great similarity of name, be assumed to be him.

Ideas, plots and themes are bound to be duplicated since there are a limited number of them, but plagiarism consists of a deliberate copying from another person's work and pretending it is your own. Again you could be taken to court if this happens.

The process of publication

Generally it takes about a year from acceptance to publication. There may be editing changes and, rewrites asked for, then the manuscript will be copy-edited, book jackets designed and the book will be promoted. The author still has quite a lot to do, apart from writing the next novel.

This will all be happening while the book is being typeset, at which stage you will have proofs to correct. This is to spot errors, not for major changes, which are expensive and for which an author can be charged. So make sure your manuscript is exactly how you want it before it is typeset.

In anticipation of publication, familiarise yourself with the main proofreading symbols, to be found in yearbooks and many books for writers.

A good editor knows her firm, what it wants and how to achieve it. Her input is immensely valuable, as she comes to the manuscript with a fresh eye, isn't as deeply enmeshed in the detail as the author and can see where changes will improve the whole. A good writer wants to be published and will comply with editorial suggestions or consider them seriously and perhaps make alternative suggestions to achieve the same objective.

After the editor has discussed or suggested changes, the copy editor will check details such as spelling, consistency and timescale.

Then the book will be sent for typesetting or, increasingly these days, set from a computer disk. Proofs will usually come as double-page spreads or bound in a paper cover, about six to four months before publication date. The author will need to go through these mainly for typing errors.

Book jackets

Meanwhile an artist will have been commissioned to design the jacket. You may or may not be asked for suggestions. Some imprints have a common format which is instantly recognisable on the shelves. You may be fortunate to be shown the jacket as it progresses from a drawing to a painting, and asked for comments.

The jackets are used for publicity before the actual books are ready. As well as the cover picture there will be the blurb on the inside front flap that you, the editor or a special department will be asked to write. This must be designed to tempt the browser into buying or borrowing your book. On a paperback the blurb will be on the outside back cover with details of the author usually on the back inside flap, Review quotes of this or earlier books will also appear.

In my survey mentioned earlier, librarians and booksellers considered jacket, blurb and title mattered a great deal when they selected books, though readers thought they mattered less. This is probably because readers tended to choose books on the basis of their familiar, favourite authors or the recommendation of friends. For the new writer's books to be in the library or bookshop, available for choice, their titles, blurbs and jackets need to be good.

Publicity in many guises

The final copies will come a month or so before publication and there is nothing to compare with the thrill of holding your first real book in your hands, unless it's holding your new baby. In many ways a book is a baby in that it has taken a long time to produce and will need constant nurturing for some time yet.

Publishers will have advertised the book, sent out review copies and tried to get your local papers, magazines and radio stations interested. The launch parties, signings in Harrods, national newspaper reviews, publicity tours and TV chat show appearances happen to very few.

Getting your own publicity

You can do a lot yourself. Some of these suggestions are expensive but others cost little more than a few postage stamps. What you do must depend on how much you can afford and whether you feel it is worth your while in terms of present sales, or publicity in the hope of future sales.

Some publicity suggestions

Make sure your publisher sends press releases to your local papers, magazines and radio stations and try to get them to interview you.

Visit local bookshops and try to persuade them to stock and display your books. If they get them they may be happy for you to sign copies.

Offer to talk to local groups. Many organisations are always eager to know about speakers, especially if you offer to do it just for expenses and a chance to sell your books at the meeting. Most publishers will be happy for you to buy books at a discount for this purpose.

Draft leaflets to send to your friends, leave in libraries or bookshops, or hand out at meetings. Typed and photocopied or printed on coloured paper they are effective, and with a computer you can illustrate them.

Throw yourself a launch party, and make sure you have copies to sell to your guests.

Have self-stick labels printed to put on your correspondence and have postcards or bookmarks printed, more or less elaborate, to give away. But do work as a team with your publisher and pass information back to them.

Reviews

Librarians and booksellers all read reviews and are influenced by them. Fewer readers read them, but they are influential.

A minute proportion of published novels is reviewed nationally, so don't expect much publicity from that. You will have more chance of a review in the local press, so cultivate your local journalists.

Regular reviewers do about one book a week, and some have little choice about which books they review. Others have complete freedom to choose. Most told me that they tend to review established authors. A reviewer told me that space is so precious authors should use any contacts they have to get reviews! It's a jungle, but if you can get in, do.

This is depressing for a new writer. A few immensely fortunate ones do get publicity at the start, but for most it's a hard slog. The only way to break in is to produce books regularly and build up a readership by word of mouth.

Money matters

You are a professional, in business and need to be businesslike in financial details.

Advances

These are the sums paid before the book is published or on publication. Don't expect a fortune the moment your book is accepted. Advances, usually between £1,000–5,000 for a first novel, are paid only on signature of contract, and often these will be split, half or a third on signature, another amount on publication, and sometimes if there are to be both hard and paperback editions, some of the advance will be retained until the second edition is out.

Royalties

Normally these are paid once or twice a year, and are sometimes a percentage of the retail price of the book. Usually the terms are 10% on hardback, less on paperback editions. If sales are high there may be a higher royalty, 12.5% or 15% on sales above a specified quantity. Sometimes with high volume sales at big discounts this may be the percentage of the publisher's receipts and, with 40% or 50% discounts to booksellers, this can be far less than authors imagine.

Royalties are often not as much as authors at first expect. The advance is set against earnings, so until the book has earned that amount you will receive no more royalties.

Where the publisher retains second rights they can earn further income by selling them. Of this you will have a share, the proportion depending on the contract, but you may only get this paid to you when the advance has been recovered. It could be a couple of years or more before you see much cash, if any more than the advance. You are not going to earn much initially.

Tax

You may be liable for tax if your income, from writing or other sources, is high enough. You can save a great deal by offsetting your expenses, but get expert advice on which of these expenses are tax-deductible. Capital expenditure, for example the purchase of a computer, may be treated in a different way to other expenses such as stationery and postage.

Even though you do not earn a great deal from your writing at first, employing an accountant who is a specialist – and not all are accustomed to the oddities of an author's finances – can save you money.

If you have another job where tax and insurance contributions are already deducted, or if you work part time, do contract work or occasional lectures, for instance, your tax affairs can become very complicated.

Make a preliminary list of accountants who specialise in helping writers, ready to approach one when it becomes advisable. The Society of Authors has leaflets and articles in their magazine, which are updated frequently as the tax laws change, and can put you in touch with accountants.

Public lending right

This is a government-funded scheme to compensate writers for library borrowings. Payment is made every February based on the loans from libraries in the previous year. Now that many library authorities are computerised there are more sample libraries than there used to be.

You need to register each edition of your book, (hardback, paperback, large print) for PLR by the end of June each year. Audio books are covered by a different Act of Parliament, and unfortunately are not eligible for lending rights.

Expenses

Most of your expenses incurred in writing are chargeable against tax, so keep good records. Obtain and file receipts wherever possible. Keep a notebook diary of when you incurred costs such as those involved in travelling to do research, mileage if you drive, parking charges, or bus and train fares, and meals out. You will have incurred many other expenses, especially during your research, in buying books and magazines, society and library subscriptions, entrance fees, photocopying, photographs and tapes.

At home you will have stationery, postage and telephone charges, perhaps an Internet rental, as well as capital expenditure such as a computer, a desk and filing materials. You will be able to claim a proportion of heating and lighting costs, but don't set aside one room as an office only, since that may affect capital gains tax when selling your house. Keep the details in case you are asked to prove your claims.

You will also have to account for your income. Again keep records. Some people maintain separate bank accounts to isolate writing income and expenditure, but often small purchases such as magazines or stamps are paid for in cash and it can be a problem to keep these expenses separate. Besides, banks may charge more for what they see as a business account.

Finally

Keep a diary of when and where you send the typescript. Allow three months for a reply, though most UK agents and publishers try to respond as soon as possible.

Persevere

First novels do not achieve tremendous success very often. Either give up, or be determined to show them you can succeed.

Questions to answer and things to do

1. Is your typescript laid out in double spacing, a clear and easily readable font, with wide margins and the pages numbered and with some identifying label such as your name and the title?

2. Have you by now got a current yearbook? You need this when you are about to send out to agents, since they change and move, and there are new ones setting up in business.

3. Have you paid special attention to your synopsis and query letter?

4. Do you understand the main points about copyright, libel and plagiarism?

5. Have you another project to start while you are waiting for replies? Agents can be very busy and may take several weeks to reply. You need to be writing something else meanwhile.

6. Be prepared for rejection, and persevere.

Tips by example

Sample query letter

Annie Author

Lavender Cottage

High Street

Whitepool

Norks.

Tel/Fax 01234 56789

E-mail Annieauthor@internetbox.com

February 14th 2005

Gloria Moneymaker
New Force Literary Agency
Keane Street
LONDON W1

Dear Gloria Moneymaker,

My friend Angela Toogood, who is one of your authors, has advised me to contact you to ask whether you would consider accepting me as a client. I am thirty years old, a former banker but now at home with young children. I have had several short stories published in women's magazines, and won one short story competition run by a regional Arts Council.

Now I have written a historical novel, 100,000 words long, set in the 1950s and featuring three schoolfriends who all face problems with their families. Marion's father has made money on the black market and wants her to marry well, but she insists on working and falls in love with Bill, a man who has plans she dislikes. About to marry someone else she realises her mistake and they are reconciled. Peggy's father is reported missing during the war so she travels to France and eventually finds his grave, which allows her to move on. Jennifer, eager to go to university, has to leave school and take a job. She falls in love with Bill, but when he deserts her for Marion she goes to University as a mature student and becomes an academic.

I enclose a more detailed synopsis and the first three chapters plus sae and look forward to your reply.

Yours sincerely,

Annie Author

Key points

1. Choose publishers and/or agents carefully.
2. Make a professional approach.
3. Pay great attention to your query letter and synopsis.
4. Send in a padded bag with return label and postage.
5. Read your contract carefully and get advice.
6. Be aware of copyright, libel and plagiarism issues.
7. Be ready to generate your own publicity.
8. Keep accounts of all your expenses.
9. Persevere, and believe in yourself.

Appendix

by Susanne McDadd

But isn't that my publisher's job...?

So you've finally managed to get your book published. Now you just have to sit back and wait to become rich and famous. Wrong.

Getting your book onto the bookshelves is just the first step. Unless the book-buying public knows it's there, the shelf is where it will stay – or, worse still, it will be returned to the dark recesses of the distributor's warehouse only to reappear in some bargain basement with a 99p sticker on it (that's if you're lucky).

Your book is competing with thousands of other books – now well past the old 100,000-a-year quota. Image the editor of the *Mail* or the *FT* opening the first of their 17 sacks of books a day and you realise that your book – or the publicity surrounding it – has to be pretty special to stand out. Book-buyers are not psychic, so, no matter how good your book is, unless something has happened to make them aware of it, they will not seek it out. All marketing activity is designed to build awareness and create the elusive word-of-mouth which is the best recommendation your book can have.

Those lucky authors commanding 6-figure advances (where royalties have become irrelevant) may have less incentive to publicise their books, and their publishers (who need to get their money back) will have more. But the majority of authors, whose publishers do not have a huge (or any) promotional budget, should be prepared to roll up their sleeves and get actively involved with the business of publicity.

What you can do: general principles

There are several things you can do in tandem with your publisher to help sell more copies of your book. The key phrase here is 'in tandem' – lone operators end up scoring own goals. NB These tips are aimed at authors of trade books, as technical, academic or professional books require different marketing techniques.

Think positive. Smaller publishers are known for their enthusiasm and flexibility but sometimes the trade-off is efficiency (not that the conglomerates are totally efficient either). You can be sure that, at some stage, something can and will go wrong – perhaps you are landed with an enthusiastic but junior publicist who sends out a rough draft of a press release, or books end up being late for an event.

However frustrated you are, be pragmatic and avoid blaming. Do not be like the author who received a coveted invitation to address sales reps and other publishing staff at his publisher's sales conference and, instead of enthusing them about his book, wasted the opportunity by castigating them about their performance instead. His message certainly had an impact but perhaps not the one he expected.

Get to know the people you will be working with (your sales and publicity contacts as well as your editor – unless they are one and the same) and ask them how you can best help. Remember that sometimes the most junior employee can be doing something important for your book so don't be too grand to learn their name.

Think laterally. The retailing explosion of the last few years means that books are sold not just in bookshops but in almost any kind of outlet – supermarkets, garden centres, museums, the internet (including your publisher's website and your own, if you have one), petrol stations, mail-order catalogues, by all kinds of organisations (e.g., charities, cultural institutes, motoring organisations) via their membership. Even motorbike shops if you've written a book about bikers. Don Shaw, author of *The Hike,* took this advice literally in helping publicise his book, with the result that even his local deli ended up stocking it.

Play to your strengths. Are you best at writing articles, speaking on the radio, giving talks or meeting the public at informal events? If you are inexperienced in any of these areas, set your hurdles low to begin with and build up confidence.

Remember the audience. Media outlets are not primarily a channel for you to publicise your book. They are there to inform and/or entertain their audiences. So put yourself in their shoes and think about how they might benefit from you or your book. Remember, different publications have different kinds of readers. You will need to adapt your article for each publication, tailoring the tone, content and angle to suit the tastes of that particular audience. For example, if your book is about plastic surgery, you would write a very different article for *Cosmopolitan* than for *The Lady*. And you would use a different kind of writing for the internet than for print. The same is true of broadcast media – think about the difference between the content of such programmes as GMTV and Question Time.

Work with your publisher. Always work in tandem with your publicist, sales manager and/or local sales rep. Run your ideas past them – duplication makes everybody look stupid. Also, you need to understand the whole thrust of the campaign. For example, you might feel proud of having agreed an exclusive article with a national newspaper but this might undermine the serialisation rights your publisher has just negotiated.

What you can do: specifics

- **The author questionnaire (AQ).** Filling this in is the first stage in marketing your book. If your publisher does not thrust an AQ at you right after you have signed your contract, this is an early warning sign that you will need to be the driving force in the marketing of your book. Some publishers, of course, ask some of these questions at the stage you submit your book, before it is accepted for publication, but it's a good idea to revisit them and gather all the information together at this stage.

  The publishing equivalent of a tax return, the AQ is designed to inform your publisher of anything that will help them sell more books. It asks you to list contacts, think of target publications/television/radio/websites, list local bookshops and connections, think of lateral sales possibilities, write author and book blurbs (*aka* author biog and cover copy).

Most publishers are stretched for time. The less time your publisher has, the fewer lateral ideas are generated, resulting in fewer marketing hits – and by extension sales. So the more thought you put into your AQ, the more your sales and marketing campaign will benefit. A few tips:

- Be thorough when writing your author and book blurbs as this information is likely to creep into later press and sales material.
- When listing target publications, websites, etc, give as much detail as possible – specific sections as well as ideas about how your book might be used (for a news item, review, reader offer, opinion piece?)
- If you have any ideas for articles related to your book, list them and the outlets for which they might be suitable.
- Do you know any high-profile, popular and relevant figures who might endorse your book?
- What are your book's selling points? Why should a bookshop stock it? What other similar books are there and how does your book differ from them? (Please do not airbrush other books from your thinking – far better to damn with faint praise.)

The AQ will be used as the basis to generate cover copy, the information sheet, press release and 'About the Author' sheet. Ask to see the drafts to ensure you are happy with the content before they are sent out.

Author photos. You will need to supply your publisher with a good, human, photograph of yourself for use on publicity materials and to give out to the press. (A passport mugshot won't do.) An electronic version is the most useful and for print purposes the best format is a high-resolution Jpeg (a minimum of 300dpi at the size the photo will be used). If you can't supply the photo electronically, a good-quality colour photographic print will do. If the photo has been taken professionally, make sure the photographer is credited whenever the photo is used. If the photographer retains copyright (which is usually the case unless otherwise agreed), permission to use the photo and payment of a fee may be necessary.

Bookshops/local events. Bookshop buying patterns have changed fundamentally. With centralised buying on the increase, sales reps who maintain a personal selling link between publisher and local bookshops are becoming a thing of the past for all but the largest publishers. Even Random House chopped several of its sales reps in August 2005.

Publishers may say that their reps call on 'Ottakars, Waterstones, Blackwells and Books Etc' – but when you probe a little, you are likely to find that the branches called on are a small proportion of that chain's total number. And getting smaller. This means that, in your local area, you effectively become the sales rep.

Your publisher will process the orders but you can be of great help in raising awareness of your book – introducing yourself, asking about events or signings, turning your book face out on shelves (as opposed to spine-out) and charming them into taking a poster or a showcard (which your publisher will provide).

A few ground-rules in approaching bookshops:

- Don't cold call. Ask your publisher to draw up a list of bookshops in your geographical area and to write to them ahead of your visit, enclosing the all-important Advance Information sheet (AI) and perhaps an 'About the Author' sheet as well. The Booksellers' Association has a useful spreadsheet or labels service, which at £12 per 100 addresses is hardly going to break the bank (Tel: 020 7802 0802/E-mail: *mail@booksellers.org.uk*).
- Publishers' mailings tend to get filed in the bin so take more copies of the AI and 'About the Author' sheet with you to the bookshop as well as a digitalcolour print-out of your book cover (which you will need to extract from your publisher).
- Maximise your chances by avoiding busy periods (lunchtimes and evenings) and by not being too pushy. Be civilised to everybody – the person manning the till in a small bookshop may well be the shop's owner.
- Don't forget libraries, which also hold events.

- Give a good reason why the bookshop should hold your event: e.g., you have lots of friends and family who will come; you belong to a society or organisation; you are well known in the area.

Events need to be supported by publicity material such as flyers and/or posters – your publisher and the bookshop or library should liaise as to who is doing what. No publicity material means no awareness, resulting in a toe-curling evening when the shop or library staff have to pretend they are customers to eke out the numbers.

Local media

National publicity is every author's dream but unless you have specific contacts, this area of activity will usually be down to your publisher.

Your main focus should be regional newspapers, local radio and events. You have a built-in advantage with local publicity outlets in that the local angle is all-important. Local, however, does not need to be restricted to your current area – think of any other local connections, such as where you were born or any area of importance in your book. Then your publicist can send out separate 'local' press releases.

The press. Your publicist will have extensive review lists of the national press and the key regionals but you should be the expert on the minutiae of local publications.

Start by collecting samples of your local newspapers and magazines. Then look for sections in which your book might be featured. A publisher's letter which shows that they have read the publication and understand its readers' interests will have a higher hit rate than the standard 'this book is wonderful, please publicise it'.

Then put all this information into electronic format – an Excel spreadsheet rather than a Word document, if possible, so that your publisher can run off labels and mailmerges. Include as much information as possible – the relevant contact, address, phone number and e-mail – and a suggestion of possible angles.

Remember that glossy magazines have longer leadtimes than newspapers, so start with them.

Websites and e-zines (electronic magazines) are another form of print outlet, the coverage of which will almost certainly be entirely down to you. Are there any local websites or associations with e-zines that might feature a review of your book? Ask your publisher to send you an electronic cover image (a low-res Jpeg or PDF format is best) and you are on your way. Even if they can't be persuaded to include a review on their site, perhaps they could be persuaded to include a link to your publisher's website or to your Amazon listing.

Opinion-formers. Another variation on the 'not what you know but who you know' theme. Let your publisher know if there are any high-profile figures living locally who might be interested in receiving a copy of your book and perhaps reviewing it for the local or national press. After all, what have you got to lose – they can only say 'no'.

Radio. Start by listening to your local radio station to get a feel for the different presenters. The BBC website (*www.bbc.co.uk*) also lists each local radio station, with varying information on programmes and presenters. Narrow down the radio station to one or two particular slots and then think of ideas and angles that might work for them.

- Unlike book reviews, radio wants a good story and how well your book is written is secondary. Ask yourself why a producer should prefer your book rather than another on the same topic.
- For non-fiction books, identify a problem and show how your book provides the solution.
- For fiction, the 'hook' could be that the book is topical either in terms of subject, location, timing or you yourself (remember that 'About the Author' sheet?) Or perhaps it shows how your readers can learn from understanding fictional relationships (e.g., abusive relationships).

Once you have secured an interview, you need to maximise the impact of your radio slot.

- Make sure that you or your publisher has sent flyers to all bookshops in the area covered by the radio station.
- Consider giving a copy of your book away as a competition prize. If there is time, get your publisher to post two or three copies to the station. Ask the presenter first and set a ridiculously easy question – something intriguing and preferably with a sense of fun to it.
- Send a flyer to the radio station reception telling them that you are booked on a particular programme and that the flyer contains all the information they will need to answer listener's queries. Leave the same flyer with the producer and the presenter.
- You should also consider highlighting specific areas of your book (with page references) to the producer or presenter.

This recognises that not they might be too busy to read the book thoroughly, and need some help, although some presenters do read every book from cover to cover. (Judi Spiers of BBC Radio Devon and formerly at BBC Radio 2 FM is a good example of a well-prepared and thoughtful broadcaster who does this).

And, finally, for the interview itself:

- BBC Radio Leicester presenter John Florance advises that authors call the station a couple of days before the interview and ask the presenter to e-mail a list of the areas that they intend to ask you about. Make up a series of questions based on these areas and practise the interview with a friend, answering the questions out loud and making a rough note of what you say. Then try to improve on your answers. Short, pithy phrases that stick in your listeners' mind are what you are after. John also stressed that 'asking for an email of the actual questions often doesn't get you far. I always find that working down a list of pre-written questions makes for boring radio' and he is quite right. Spontaneity is all.
- If you feel you need a safely net, jot down key points on a piece of card (not paper as it could rustle).

- People often speak faster when they are nervous, so guard against gabble. (Recording the mock interview and listening to it will help you gauge this.)
- Smile as you talk – it helps make you sound more relaxed.
- Be passionate about your book. If you don't seem to care about it why should anyone else? Don't worry about people disagreeing with you, that's what makes good radio.
- Think of yourself as the co-host of the programme. Be bold, take control of the interview at times. Make sure you use the host's name regularly and get the radio station's name right (it's easy to get muddled when you are doing several interviews in one day).
- Be prepared to talk about what is *not* in your book. Author and regular broadcaster Graham Lawler, in promoting his book *Mathematics for Adults,* used the headline, 'Why we are all heading for economic meltdown' and talked about the financial state of the country. His book sold over a thousand copies in the first three weeks of publication – not bad for a maths book!
- Local knowledge is essential. For instance, on BBC Wiltshire Sound, you have to be careful when talking about processed food – there is a well-known meat processor with factories in Wiltshire and many listeners will have family who work there. If you don't know the area, ask the producer whether there are any sensitivities you should know about before you go on air.
- Mention of your book should form a natural part of the conversation but presenters don't always make this easy so it's up to you. Without going over the top, try to find different ways of mentioning the fact that you are an author and, most importantly, the title of your book. For example in a radio interview, Graham Lawler said: 'I wrote my book, *Mathematics for Adults,* because of the numbers of adults who were asking me for help', and 'When I was researching my book, *Mathematics for Adults,* it became clear to me that many people would benefit from using powerful but devastatingly simple skills that anyone can master.'

Look at how powerful these statements are, and how using them in an interview helps create interest in your book.

- Whatever you do, avoid the direct plug as in 'My book on *'Mathematics for Adults'* is published this week by Studymates at £9.99 and is available from all good bookshops.' This will have presenters vowing never to have you on the show again. They want value from you, not to be treated as a means to an end! If you are prepared to take part in a real, interesting exchange of views, you are likely to get a plug in any case – and not be blacklisted!
- Never disagree head-on with a presenter. Use strategies like, 'I can see why you say that but there is another viewpoint. Have you ever considered...?'
- Listen to the way other guests field questions and/or arouse interest in their book.
- Finally, remember that a good radio interview is a conversation between two or more people with the audience overhearing what is going on – so, whatever you do, *never* read on air.

Talks. Alongside the bookshop and library events mentioned earlier, check out whether there are any other potential outlets for talks – schools, clubs etc. And always ensure that you have copies of your book with you for the audience to buy. Many people will buy a book at the end of an interesting talk but won't bother to go to a bookshop later when the memory of the evening has faded. For smaller venues, you may need to chase your publisher to make sure delivery of the books are organised – or you might just have to take a box yourself.

Book launches. A book launch is not necessarily essential to the success of your book but, having achieved publication, you may feel you deserve one! Be clear about who you expect to attend, who is paying and what you expect such an event to achieve. If, for example, you want to get write-ups in the press, sending out review copies and press releases may be just as effective. Free wine and nibbles is no guarantee that journalists will give you column inches. However, if you are a good conversationalist and advocate for your work and can supply 'added value' by meeting the journalists in person, this should be your goal on the night.

Don Shaw held his launch as a ticketed event at the exquisite Tissington Hall in Derbyshire – and persuaded over 100 people to pay for the privilege of buying his book, with the profits from the event going to charity. But Don – a BAFTA award-winning screenwriter – was well known in Derbyshire, so this was an exception. For novice authors, a more realistic approach (assuming you have family and friends you can rope in to attend as insurance against a poor turnout) would be to hold your launch at a bookshop and persuade your publisher to make a small contribution. You will need to check that showcards advertising the event are prominently displayed in the shop, that there is no confusion as to who is paying for what and that the local press have been invited.

Amazon. Amazon is taking a growing share of the book-buying market and has a policy of stocking all books published. Obviously, the more information you can give about your book, the better, as browsers are unlikely to buy simply on the basis of a book's title and bibliographic details. As a minimum they need to see the cover, a blurb about the book and the author. Better still would be a detailed contents list and sample chapter, together with author and publisher reviews.

Check out your book on Amazon and nag your publisher remorselessly until all relevant material is posted! There is also a section where authors can post their own further notes.

Longer term

Publicity works best when launch-centred publicity is combined with longer-term effort. Securing a regular newspaper, magazine or column, after which you can credit your book, is one idea. Articles in magazines – again with the all-important credit – is another.

If your book is of the relevant genre, getting onto the festival circuit can be helpful in building up word-of-mouth – start contacting them as early as possible, as festivals tend to book their authors up far in advance (up to a year for the larger festivals).

For a free list of festivals, try the British Council website http://literaryfestivals.britishcouncil.org. For a printed version, send an SAE to: Laura Costello, Web and Information Officer, Film and Literature Department, British Council, 10 Spring Gardens, London SW1A 2BN.

Finally

The key to marketing your book in tandem with smaller publishers is to forget about the kind of promotion household-name authors might get and instead take pride in 'guerrilla' marketing and the accumulation of small-scale publicity hits. Work with your publisher in getting the initial marketing material right, be your own research assistant – not to mention rep – and above all be positive and try to have fun.

Susanne McDadd,

Susanne McDadd is the founder of *www.Publishing-Services.co.uk,* which provides umbrella services for smaller publishers and authors.

© Susanne McDadd 2005.

Glossary

Acceptance
an offer to publish the manuscript.

Advance
money given to an author by a publisher on signing a contract to write a book and/or on delivery of script and publication of that book.

Agent
a person or company that acts on an author's behalf, selling the author's work and negotiating fees. Agents take a percentage of authors' earnings.

Allowable expenses
those expenses on machinery, equipment and essential requirements an author has in order to work, which can be offset against income before income tax is charged.

Antagonist
character who is opposed to the protagonist.

Blurb
a summary of the book, which is printed on the back cover or on the first page of a book, and designed to attract readers.

Book jacket
the outer cover of the book, usually with an illustration.

Category fiction
books/fiction of a particular type, e.g. romance or science fiction, which are published as a regular series and have similarities within the series such as length, style and conventions.

CDs
Compact disks, on which vast amounts of data, including audio and video, can be stored electronically.

Characters
the people who feature in your novel.

Cliffhanger	an exciting unresolved situation usually at the end of a scene or chapter.
Conflict	some disagreement, aims that are not compatible.
Contract	the terms agreed by author and publisher, covering such matters as payment, publication, ownership of second rights and proportions of earnings allocated under these.
Copy-editing	checking and altering a writer's work for the house style of the publisher and for consistency and grammar.
Copyright	the legal rights an author/publisher has over their work, so that no one can copy all or part of the work without the author's or publisher's permission.
Criticism	a detailed appraisal of a piece of writing.
Critique group	a group of writers who meet to criticise (hopefully constructively) work of members. Groups usually comprise amateur writers, but published writers do join.
Deadline	the date by which a writer aims to complete or submit a script.
Deus ex machina	'the god from the machine', an unexpected event which solves an apparently impossible situation.
Dialect	the words peculiar to one region or area of a country.
Dialogue	conversation, or the words spoken by characters.
Disk	a device for storing computer programmes and data.

Double spacing	lines typed to give approximately three lines per inch on a typescript (single spacing gives six).
Draft	a version, usually the first uncorrected or unpolished thoughts.
DVDs	similar to CDs, but holding much more data.
Edition	a book may be published in different format, each one is a separate edition.
Editor	the person who commissions writers for books/articles/plays and who sees the project through to the final printing and distribution.
Editing	checking on accuracy, consistency, relevance, structure, and generally preparing a piece of writing for publication.
E-mail	electronic mail, a method of communicating with others via the Internet. Each user worldwide has a unique address.
Enquiry (or query) letter	letter to the editor outlining what an author has written, how long it is and why it might be of interest to the publisher.
Exposition	an explanation of events or feelings or actions in a novel, usually done by narrative, not dialogue.
Flashback	portrayal of a scene from the past as if it were taking place now.
Flash forward	putting in a scene from the future, or a brief foretelling of what is still to come.

Foreshadowing	hinting, or laying down the clues for something that is to happen later in the book.
Font	a style and size of type, eg italic 10.
Genre	a type of book, e.g. crime, fantasy, historical, literary, romantic, saga, science fiction, western.
Hardback	where the cover of the book is stiff.
Hard copy	paper print-out of text as opposed to a display on a computer screen.
Hook	the means by which a writer obtains the reader's attention and interest.
House style	every publisher/magazine will have certain ways of writing things, for example standardising on spellings such as the use of 'ise' instead of 'ize' at the end of words like criticise.
Imagery	use of metaphorical language.
Internet	a link, via a computer and telephone line, to other computers for correspondence, information or exchange of ideas.
ISPs	Internet Service Providers are companies which provide, amongst other services, access to the Internet.
Large print	editions of a book in a large typeface, intended to make reading easier for people with eyesight problems.
Layout	the way the writing is set out on the page, with margins, line spacing and headings.
Libel	a false, damaging statement published in permanent form.

Living history museum	a place where the past is recreated, usually with people dressed in the costume of the time who explain things to visitors.
Manuscript/script/ typescript	an author's typed/word-processed piece of work.
Market	any place where a writer's work may be sold.
Metaphor	a non-literal use of language to suggest a comparison.
Modifiers	words which qualify, change or restrict others.
Moral rights	the rights of paternity, i.e. having one's authorship recognised, and of integrity, i.e. not having the work changed in a 'derogatory' manner. These rights have to be asserted in writing by the author.
Multiple submissions	sending work to more than one agent or publisher at a time.
Narrative	the telling of a story.
Networking	forming connections with other people who have the same professional interests.
Online	a connection to another computer or service.
Pace	the speed of progress, whether fast or slow, smooth or jerky, of a piece of writing.
Paperback	where the cover of the book is flexible card or thick paper.
Partials	part of a book which the publisher likes to see, in order to judge whether to read the rest with a view to publication.

Plagiarism	deliberately to copy another writer's ideas such as plot and characters and use them as your own.
Plot	a series of happenings connected by cause and effect.
Polishing	checking a manuscript to make final changes and corrections.
Presentation	the way in which a manuscript is shown to an editor.
Program	the system by which a computer receives and deals with data.
Proofreading	final check of proofs for typos, spelling mistakes, missing text and so on.
Proofs	typeset book which is corrected for printing.
Proof marks	the symbols used to indicate changes needed.
Protagonist	one of the leading characters.
Pseudonym	a name used by an author that is not his own – a pen name.
Public Lending Right	money an author gets each time his book is borrowed from a library. The author must register for PLR at the time of publication.
Re-enactment	societies specialising in recreating life in the past, such as battles.
Rejections	when an agent or publisher declines to handle or buy a typescript. There are many reasons for rejection apart from the quality of the work.
Remainders	the books that are left after sales have fallen off are remaindered – offered to

	the author at a cheap rate and to cheap book shops.
Research	discovering and verifying facts which may be used in or as background for the novel.
Review	a report, usually in the media, assessing a book.
Revising	checking a piece of writing and making changes to it, including making sure the facts are accurate.
Rewriting	changing a piece of writing, sometimes radically, sometimes with only minor alterations.
Rights	legal rights of an author in terms of the sale of a piece of work.
Royalties	a percentage of the selling price of a book that goes to the author after publication, based on the numbers sold or the monies received.
Search directory	a device for finding information on the Internet, organised on a 'tree and branch' system.
Search engine	another Internet searching device, which will locate websites identified by a phrase or word.
Second rights	editions of a book or article after the first publication, e.g. paperback, large print, translation, syndication, extracts, anthologies, adaptations for radio or TV or film.
Shape	the form and pattern of the novel.
Simile	a comparison, a figure of speech comparing things using 'as' or 'like'.

Softback	see paperback.
Solicited script	work an editor has asked to see.
Spellchecker	a computer spelling tool, which can highlight errors and often suggest alternative words.
Sub-editing	checking copy for house style, accuracy, consistency, spelling, grammar and so on.
Submissions	the manuscripts sent to editors for consideration, in the hope of acceptance.
Sub-plot	a minor, subsidiary plot in a novel.
Synonym	a word with the same or a similar meaning as another word.
Synopsis	A summary of a piece of writing.
Theme	a subject of a novel, often an abstract quality.
Thesaurus	a book which gives alternative words of the same or similar meaning, and where concepts are grouped.
Title page	cover sheet of manuscript.
Trade paperback	a book with a flexible cover, but usually of a larger format and higher price than the conventional paperback.
Typos	typing errors on the manuscript or galleys.
Typesetting	putting a piece of writing into the typeface, size and in the appropriate space the publisher uses.
Unsolicited	work sent on spec to an agent or editor.

URL	Uniform Resource Locator, the address of a website.
VAT	Value Added Tax, imposed on almost all purchases, which can be reclaimed by persons registered under the scheme.
Voice	the particular individual style of a writer.
Website	pages set up by individuals, organisations and companies to advertise, impart information or sell items.
Word processing	using a computer in order to type work, and then being able to manipulate information by inserting, deleting, moving text, changing the layout and many more processes.
World Wide Web	the system of websites connected by the Internet.
Writer's block	when a writer cannot continue, through lack of ideas, motivation, exhaustion or psychological difficulties.
Yearbook	a reference book published annually, such as *The Writers' and Artists' Yearbook* or *The Writer's Handbook*.

Further reading and reference

Magazines for writers

The Author, The Society of Authors, 84 Drayton Gardens, London SW10 9SB . Tel 0202 7373 6642. Magazine for members, but individual copies can be bought. www.societyofauthors.org

The Bookseller, Endeavour House, 5th Floor, 189 Shaftsbury Avenue, London, WC2H 8TJ. Tel 020 7420 6006. Main journal for the book trade. www.thebookseller.com

Historical Novel Review, Historical Novel Society and *Solander* both magazines of the Historical Novel Society. See below for membership details.

Mslexia PO Box 656, Freepost NEA5566, Newcastle uopn Tyne, NE1 1BR.

Writers' Forum, Writers International Ltd, PO Box 3229, Bournemouth, BH1 1ZS. Tel 01392 2113894 www.writers-forum.com

Writing Magazine, and *Writers' News* Writers News Ltd, PO Box 168, Wellington Street, Leeds, W. Yorks. LS1 1RF. Tel 0113 238 8333. www.writersnews.co.uk

Books

This is just a selection, there are many more. Second-hand copies of the annual publications can often be obtained at a fraction of the cost of new editions and may serve your purposes quite adequately.

Reference books – general, on writing and publishing

Writers' and Artists' Yearbook, A. & C. Black, Lists publishers and magazines, plus advice on various aspects of writing and publishing.

The Writer's Handbook, Barry Turner, Macmillan Reference Books. Another yearbook with lists and information.

Writer's Market, Reader's Digest Books, USA. A similar yearbook of American information.

Writing TV Scripts Successful Writing in 10 Weeks Steve Welton Studymates.

The Author's Handbook, David Bolt, Piatkus Books.

Authors by Profession volume 2, Victor Bonham-Carter, Bodley Head. Volume 1 from the Society of Authors.

From Pitch to Publication, Carole Blake, Macmillan. An agent's account of her work.

Inside Book Publishing, Giles N. Clark, Blueprint. A career builder's guide.

An Author's Guide to Publishing, Michael Legat, Robert Hale.

Publishing and Bookselling in the Twentieth Century, F. A. Mumby, Unwin Hayman.

Writers' Questions Answered, Gordon Wells, Allison & Busby.

The Writer's Rights, Michael Legat, A. & C. Black.

Kate Walker's 12 Point, Guide to Writing Romance Studymates.

Reference books – useful to purchase

Many of the larger multi-volume books such as encyclopaedias and dictionaries are now available on CD-ROM. There are many similar titles to the ones mentioned. Shop around until you find those which suit your needs and pocket.

Brewer's Concise Dictionary of Phrase and Fable, Helicon.

Brewer's Dictionary of Names, People, Places and Things, Helicon.

Chambers Dictionary of Synonyms and Antonyms, Larousse.

Collins What Happened When, Helicon.

Collins English Spelling Dictionary, Helicon.

The Elements of Style, William Strunk Jr. and E. B. White, Macmillan Publishing Co New York.

Encyclopaedia of Dates and Events, Teach Yourself Books, Hodder & Stoughton.

How to Write Historical Novels, Michael Legat, Allison & Busby.

The Internet Guide for Writers, Malcolm Chisolm, How To Books.

The Internet: A Writer's Guide Jane Dormer, A. & C. Black.

Interviewing Techniques for Writers and Researchers, Susan Dunne, A. & C. Black 1995.

The Nuts and Bolts of Writing, Michael Legat, Robert Hale.

Research for Writers, Ann Hoffman, A. & C. Black. This is a wonderful compilation of where to find almost any information you need.

Slang Down the Ages, Jonathon Green, Kyle Cathie.

Starting to Write, Marina Oliver and Deborah Oliver, How To Books 1996, 2nd ed, Tudor House 2003.

Surfing on the Internet, J. C. Herz, Little Brown, 1995.

Twenty Master Plots, Ronald B. Tobias, Piatkus.

Writing a Novel, Marina Oliver, How To Books 1996, 4th Edition 2006.

Writing Historical Fiction, Rhona Martin, A. & C. Black, 1995.

Writing Romantic Fiction, Marina Oliver, How To Books, 1997.

Books mainly for consultation in libraries

Army, Navy and Air Force lists.

Bibliographical Index will tell you if a bibliography exists on any subject.

British Autobiographies, William Matthews, up to 1951.

British Diaries, 1442–1942, William Matthews.

British Historical Statistics B. R. Mitchell, CUP, Cambridge 1988.

British National Bibliography for published works.

Buildings of England series Nicholas Pevsner.

Cambridge Biographical Encyclopaedia.

Chambers Biographical Dictionary.

Chronology of History, 4 volumes or on CD-ROM.

Chambers Dictionary of Spelling, Larousse.

Concise Dictionary of English Idioms, B. A. Pythian, Hodder & Stoughton.

Concise Dictionary of English Slang, B. A. Pythian, Hodder & Stoughton.

Concise Dictionary of Phrase and Fable, B. A. Pythian, Hodder & Stoughton.

Concise Oxford Dictionary of Proverbs, Oxford University Press.

Dictionary of National Biography, 31 volumes but also available on CD-ROM.

Dictionary of Slang, Jonathon Green, Cassell.

Gascoigne Encyclopaedia of Britain, Macmillan.

A History of the Cost of Living, J. Burnett, Penguin.

Historical Facts Series, 6 volumes from 1485–1985, Macmillan.

Hutchinson Dictionary of Biography, Helicon.

Hutchinson Pocket Fact Finder, Helicon.

Natural Phenomena and Chronology of the Seasons, E. J. Lowe, of events AD220–1753.

Oxford Dictionary of Quotations, Oxford University Press.

Penguin Dictionary of Historical Slang, Eric Partridge, Penguin.

Penguin Dictionary for Writers and Editors, Penguin.

Prices and Wages in England from the 12th to the 19th Century, by Lord Beveridge and others.

Punctuation Made Easy in One Hour, Graham King, Mandarin.

Song Index for songs up to 1934, and *Popular Song* Index to present day.

Song Catalogue of the BBC Music Library Catalogue of Holdings.

They Saw it Happen series.

World Historical Fiction Guide.

Whitacker's Almanack, J. Whitaker & Sons, Ltd.

Who Was Who, in 9 volumes plus index. A. & C. Black.

Websites on the internet of value to writers

There are millions of websites, and hundreds of these have information of use to writers, hundreds if not thousands with information of use to historians. They are being added to, deleted, sold and changed every day, so I have concentrated on a few which are more general, with lots of links to other sites, or which I have found especially interesting. Most publishers have them, so do many authors.

www.pro.gov.uk This is the UK Public Records Office.

www.bl.uk is the British Library site with many links of interest.

www.bbc.co.uk/education has many useful articles and links.

www.bodley.ox.ac.uk/boris/guides/maps The Oxford University Library, has many illustrated historical maps.

www.andromeda.rutgers.edu/~jlynch/writing/ has much useful advice on writing, plus lots of links to eighteenth century sources.

www.zuzu.com has many links.

www.calltoarms.com is the site with information on re-enactment groups.

www.historicalnovelsociety.org has much of interest about historical novels.

www.storytracks.net is the manuscript appraisal agency I help to run.

www.marina-oliver.net is my own website with details of my books and a few extracts.

Useful addresses

British Document Supply Centre at Boston Spa, Wetherby, West Yorkshire, LS23 7BQ for inter-library loans of books, films and fiches. Access through your local library or direct 01937 546138.

British Library, 96 Euston Road, London, NW1 2DB. www.bl.uk

Call to Arms, 1 Lyng Lane, North Lopham, Diss, Norfolk. IP22 2HR. 01953 681676, e-mail admin@calltoarms.com and URL www.calltoarms.com publishes a comprehensive international directory of re-enactment societies, with details of membership, specialisations and types of activities.

Historical Novel Society, Membership Secretary, 38 The Fairway, Newton Ferrars, Devon. PL8 1DP. www.historicalnovelsociety.org For readers as well as writers. Magazine, reviews.

Romance Writers of America, 13700 Veterans Memorial Drive, Suite 315, Houston, TX 77014, USA. (713) 440–6885. http://rwanational.com

The Romantic Novelists' Association, Enquiries 38 Maes y Llan, Dwygyfylchi, Penmaenmawr, Conwy. LL34 6RY. www.rna-uk.org Meetings, conferences, newsletter. Annual subscription plus reading fee for critiques of novels by unpublished members.

Public Lending Right Office, Richard House, Sorbonne Close, Stockton-on-Tees, TS17 6DA. 01642 604699. www.plr.uk.com

Public Record Office Chancery Lane, London WC2A 1LR, and Ruskin Avenue, Kew, Richmond, Surrey. TW9 4DU. 020 8876 3444.

Research Publications International, PO Box 45, Reading RG1 8HF. 01734 583247. Provides lists of available newspapers worldwide on CD-ROM or film, PO Box 45, Reading RG1 8HF.

Royal Commission on Historical Manuscripts, Quality House, Quality Court, Chancery Lane, London WC2A 1HP. Registers and keeps catalogues of private papers.

The Society of Authors, 84 Drayton Gardens, London SW10 9SB. 0202 7373 6642. www.societyofauthors.org

StorytrackS An appraisal agency the author helps to run. Coseley House, Munslow, Craven Arms, Shropshire. SY7 9ET. 01395 279659. www.storytracks.net

Books by the author mentioned or quoted in the text

Non-fiction

Write and Sell Your Novel

Novels – Writing as Marina Oliver

Midlands sagas set in the 1920s and 1930s.

*The Cobweb Cage**

*The Glowing Hours**

*The Golden Road**

Mainly 17th century novels

*Cavalier Courtship**

*Restoration Affair**

*Player's Wench**

*Sibylla & The Privateer**

*Runaway Hill**

*Lord Hugo's Wedding**

*Campaign for a Bride**

Charms of a Witch

*Strife Beyond Tamar**

*The Baron's Bride**

*Masquerade for the King**

Writing as Sally James (Regencies)

*Heir to Rowanlea**

*A Clandestine Affair**

*Petronella's Waterloo**

Writing as Livvy West

*Royal Courtship**

Her Captive Cavalier

Writing as Donna Hunt

*Forbidden Love**

* also in large print

Index

Writing TV Scripts - Successful writing in ten weeks

For published and unpublished screenwriters

Author	Steve Wetton
Foreword	Don Shaw BBC Tv's *Dangerfield* and the legendary *Z-Cars*
Price	£9.99
Format	Paperback, 215 x 135mm, 160pp
ISBN	1-84285-071-7
Publication	10 February 2005
Territory	World all language

'I would have this on my shelf as my writer's Bible, were I starting out today.' – *Don Shaw, BAFTA award-winning screenwriter (BBC TV's Dangerfield and the legendary Z-cars)*

About the Book

Written by professional screenwriter Steve Wetton – creator of the BBC's hit series 'Growing Pains' and who has written for performers such as BRIAN CONLEY, LENNY HENRY, RUSS ABBOTT, and THE TWO RONNIES – this is a passionate and generous book, which shares insider tips and techniques. Drawing on examples on well-known sit-coms, dramas and soaps – from Fawlty Towers to Friends – the book guides the aspiring screenwriter through all the stages of planning to borrowing techniques to make your script stand out to discussing the logistics of formatting and submitting scripts. He shares his experience of taking projects to pilot stage, only to have hopes dashed, and helps you learn from his successes and mistakes. Creative writing students, established TV writers and novice writers alike will benefit from this book. Other key areas covered include:

- using one script to approach different people
- how to get your script to the right person
- payments and the role of an agent
- what a scriptwriter does and does not write
- the pros and cons of writing with a partner
- how to progress your career

About the Author

Steve Wetton has written for TV for many years and also taught creative writing at Derby University and The Welsh Writer's Holiday at Caerleon.
He lives in Mackworth near Derby.

Shakespeare —The Barriers Removed

For A level support and first year undergraduates

Author   Paul Innes PhD

Price   £9.99
Format   Paperback, 215 x 135mm,
160pp
ISBN   1-84285-051-2
Publication 30 Oct 2005
Territory   World all language

In Focus - A Studymates Series

About the Book
This book makes Shakespeare accessible to a
new generation of readers interested in the
subject. It makes no assumptions about prior
knowledge of the plays and poems and places
them in their historical context.
This book is aimed at all readers for whom
there are barriers of language and cultural distance. Dr Innes provides
chapters on characterisation, genre, setting, structure, performance and
history; information that will help them untangle his works. He explains the
implications of Shakespeare's writing and performance techniques as well as
describing how criticism has treated him, from liberalism to feminism, from
psycho-analysts to materialists. This book explains:

- how to deal with genre
- setting the scene
- sub-plots, interspersing and chiamus

- the different types of character
- how to analyse text
- performing the plays and reading the poems

About the Author
Paul Innes PhD is a lecturer in Literature in the Department of Adult & Continuing
Education at Glasgow University. He has also taught at the Universities of
Stirling, Strathclyde and Edinburgh, and held a British Council Lectureship at the
University of Warsaw from 1992-95. He lives in Glasgow with his wife and two
infant children.

Kate Walker's 12-Point Guide to Writing Romance

Author	Kate Walker
ISBN	1-84285-044-X
Price	£10.99
Format	246mm x 171 mm Paperback
Extent	150 pp
Territory	World –all language

Kate Walker has come up with another keeper. A fabulous resource, ...If you write romance, do yourself a favour and get this book. You won't be disappointed.
Trish Morey (Australia)

The Book

Structured into 14 chapters, Kate Walker takes you through the 12-Points that you need to consider, to write a beautiful romance novel. The 12-point Guide explains what is meant by romance and takes you one step at a time through the process of writing emotion, and conflict.

She explains how dialogue should be natural between your heroine and her hero and explains the difference between sensuality and passion and why you need both in your novel.

Kate Walker dissects the alpha male and explains why women fall for him and shows you how to effectively plot and include the intense black moment, an essential component of your story.

Finally Kate Walker explains how to end with a believable happy ending where two people experience the sort of love that only happens once in a lifetime.

About The Author

Kate Walker has written over 40 Romance novels and sells hundreds of thousands of novels per year. Kate Walker is married and lives with her husband Stephen, in Lincolnshire, UK.

- Kate Walker is a 'name' in the world of romance and draws a huge response from readers whenever she travels.
- This title has achieved consistently high reviews in the UK, the USA and now in Australia.
- The author has written over 40 best selling romance novels selling millions of romance novels worldwide.

Understanding Maths Third Edition

Basic Mathematics Explained

Author: Graham Lawler
Price £9.99
Format Paperback, 215 x 135mm, 160pp
ISBN 1-84285-086-5
Publication March 30 2006
Territory World all language

Understanding Maths
Basic mathematics explained

About the Book

As a professional writer you have to control your business expenditure and income. Do you find it hard to cope with fractions, percentages, averages, decimals, angles, area, volume, or other number and data-related work? Then this is definitely the book for you. Written by an experienced and sympathetic mathematics teacher, it will help you master all these important skills. Whether you are just starting out as a writer or your are a professional, this book is a must. It explains in easy steps everything you need for successful number and data handling that you need to control your business as a professional writer.

Chapters include:
- **Numbers and place value,**
- **Dealing with fractions,**
- **Calculating with percentages,**
- **Working with decimals,**
- **Using a calculator,**
- **Angles and turning,**
- **Area and volume,**
- **Data handling,**
- **Probabilities and chance,**
- **Estimating and checking**

Review on Amazon.co.uk

★★★★★ **It does what it says on the cover,**

If like me you had an awful time understanding maths in school (pre 1980's) and you now need to get to grips with the subject (kids homework getting harder!) then Understanding Maths by Graham Lawler is a 'must have book'.
Wish I had this book 30 years ago.

About the Author

Graham Lawler MA is a teacher with over twenty years' experience, including as head of mathematics. In He has acted as a consultant on mathematical education for both the **BBC** and **Channel 4**, and is the author of **BBC Bitesize Maths** and broadcasts regularly on radio as 'Mr Educator'.

STUDY SKILLS Maximise your time to pass exams

Ideal for writers needing to reserach
- In Focus- A Studymates Series

Author   John Kennedy
Price   £9.99
Format   Paperback, 215 x 135mm; 160pp
ISBN   1-84285-064-4
Publication June 2005
Territory World all language

Far removed from the outdated read-and-revise model, this book gives
practical advice on how to develop the key skills needed for successful study
– at all levels **and is ideal for writers needing to research topics**. It
recognises that there are many different types of research – from writing to
summarising to planning – and is structured in self-contained units, thereby
allowing readers to meet their individual needs by focussing on their weakest
skills. Additional sections include how to deal with case studies and make
successful oral presentations.

Other key areas covered include:

- Learning how to learn

- Developing writing skills

- Reports: how to create them

- Research: how to do it effectively

- Evaluating sources

- Case studies

About the Author
John Kennedy is an expert and lecturer in communication and management
studies at the Royal Military Academy at Sandhurst in the UK. He left school
at the age of 15 with no qualifications and worked in construction as a
labourer. At one time he was also a drummer for the rock star Van Morrison
and later a trainee on Wall Street. He gained his education by patient part-
time study over a number of years and now holds an MBA degree and is a
recognised expert in communication and management.

More books from Studymates

Better French by Monique Jackman

Many people learn French for years at school, only to reach a plateau beyond which they never emerge. This book is an effective short-cut to fluency in French. Now in its third edition, *Better French* helps the intermediate reader reach fluency by showing them the right way to use 'problem' words. It addresses the subtleties of the language: Are *donc* and *alors* interchangeable? What about *grand* or *gros*? When do you use *c'est* or *il est*? When do you pronounce the final 's' in *plus*? Learning the answers to these and a host of other questions can finally steer you to success.

The Academic Essay by Dr Derek Soles

The academic essay is the mainstay of assessment from the sixth-form upwards. Yet formal training in this complex area is rarely given and students spend unnecessary time struggling to get it right

This book is a step-by-step guide to all the stages of writing an academic essay. The first part deals with gathering, evaluating and organising information; the second how to write effective introductions and concluding paragraphs, and the final section how to revise and edit your work. Full of practical tips and advice gleaned from years of experience as a tutor on the receiving end of essays, this is essential reading for every student in full- or part-time education today.